Progressive Perspective Drawing for Theatrical Scene Design

Progressive Perspective Drawing for Theatrical Scene Design provides theatrical scenic designers with the tools to create quick and precise perspective drawings.

The book explores three methods of perspective drawings at progressive skill levels – the Grid Method, the Frame Method, and the Freehand with References Method – allowing scenic designers to build on their drawing technique consistently. Replete with discussions on pencil techniques, step-by-step instructions, and set sketches from professional set design projects, this volume guides readers from the basics of the cube system to the more challenging freehand drawing.

Progressive Perspective Drawing for Theatrical Scene Design is an excellent resource for students of Scene Design, Stage Design, Set Design, Scenography, Stagecraft, and Design for Theatre, as well as an accessible self-study guide for those with an interest in scene design.

The book includes access to downloadable pre-made perspective grids, to help readers familiarize themselves with one and two vanishing point grids.

Dunsi Dai is a professional scene designer (USA Local 829) and a Professor of Scene Design at Webster University, Conservatory of Theatre Arts, USA.

Progressive Perspective Drawing for Theatrical Scene Design

Dunsi Dai

Routledge
Taylor & Francis Group
NEW YORK AND LONDON

First published 2021
by Routledge
605 Third Avenue, New York, NY 10158

and by Routledge
2 Park Square, Milton Park, Abingdon, Oxon, OX14 4RN

Routledge is an imprint of the Taylor & Francis Group, an informa business

Library of Congress Cataloging-in-Publication Data
Names: Dai, Dunsi, 1954– author.
Title: Progressive perspective drawing for theatrical scene design / Dunsi Dai.
Description: New York : Routledge, 2021. | Includes index.
Identifiers: LCCN 2020039893 (print) | LCCN 2020039894 (ebook) | ISBN 9780367860783 (hardback) | ISBN 9780367860790 (paperback) | ISBN 9781003016779 (ebook)
Subjects: LCSH: Perspective—Technique. | Theaters—Stage-setting and scenery—Design.
Classification: LCC T369 .D28 2021 (print) | LCC T369 (ebook) | DDC 792.02/5—dc23
LC record available at https://lccn.loc.gov/2020039893
LC ebook record available at https://lccn.loc.gov/2020039894

ISBN: 978-0-367-86078-3 (hbk)
ISBN: 978-0-367-86079-0 (pbk)
ISBN: 978-1-003-01677-9 (ebk)

Typeset in Gill Sans
by Apex CoVantage, LLC

Visit the eResources: www.routledge.com/9780367860790

To my wife Lan and daughter Mona

CONTENTS

PREFACE

Perspective drawing is one of the most effective ways for members of a theatrical production team to communicate with one another. Every drawing not only needs to be in perspective but also needs to be in proportion and very much "readable" with key details. This means the work needs to be drawn clearly and convincingly to represent the proposed set.

This book is for theatrical scene designers who wish to master fast-paced perspective drawing skills. It also applies to scenic design in other fields, such as for TV specials, theme park design, corporative convention design, and event design. It can be used for interior design as well.

The procedure of learning perspective drawing for scene design starts with developing a basic understanding of perspective drawing: first, by learning a basic perspective drawing unit—the cube system; then, by moving progressively into three perspective drawing methods: the Grid Method; the Frame Method; and the Freehand with References Method.

Each of these three drawing methods can stand alone. The differences among them are based on the level of challenge and required drawing skill level. In choosing which method to use to create your perspective drawing, you will be best served by tying your choice to the skill level which you feel most comfortable with. If you are at a beginning stage in drawing without much of an art training background, you may want to start with the Grid Method, which offers a complete reference system with which to start your sketch. After you feel more comfortable with perspective basics and have improved your drawing skills, you may want to progress into the next stage, the Frame Method, to speed up your drawing pace. Finally, when you feel that you are ready for the challenge, you may want to try out the Freehand with References Method, which will further speed up your drawing pace and allow you to enjoy the freedom of freehand drawing.

SOMETHING YOU MAY WANT TO KNOW BEFORE YOU START

- The cube system is the foundation for all perspective drawing methods introduced in this book.
- The Grid Method is straightforward and easy to use. It allows you to lay your drawing into a perspective grid which serves as your drawing reference. It can help a designer without much art training to start drawing scenic design sketches in perspective in short order. However, this method is on the slow side in practical terms, since you have to work out the perspective grid first before you can draw your set based on it. One way to work around this challenge is to print out a pre-made grid, put a layer of vellum over it, then draw your perspective sketch on the velum. A collection of pre-made perspective grids in PDF are loaded to the publisher's website (www.routledge.com/9780367860790), where readers can download those pre-made PDF grids for free, print them out, and put them to use.
- The most recommended way to draw a perspective drawing for scene design is the Frame Method. It is a method of setting up simple reference points, then estimating the set's perspective relationships referring to this set-up. Most of the set design sketches examples shown in this book used this method. The ideal scenario is that after you understand the perspective basics, have mastered the cube system, and become familiar with the Grid Method, you will build up some perspective drawing skills. Then, you will be able to establish perspective visions and be ready to further progress into a "freer" environment to speed up your perspective drawing pace. Using the Frame Method requires much more estimation. Some practice will be needed in order to become proficient. The promise is that once you master it, it works amazingly well and fast.
- The Freehand with References Method works well for people with much more perspective drawing experience and advanced drawing skills. It focuses on setting up a "reference" to be used to estimate the perspective relationship of the objects on the set. Making consistent estimations are expected. This allows a designer to further speed up the drawing process. It works especially well when it is applied to non-conventional theatre configurations, such as in an environmental set design. Some of the drawing examples shown in this book are done with this method.
- One chapter on recommended drawing techniques is included to offer help on ways to enhance the look of your perspective drawings. Although scenic designers need to draw set sketches clearly first and foremost for good communication, it helps designers to make their design sketches look handsome, which will help to "sell" their design ideas. A good-looking

sketch tends to make your production team get excited about your design and eager to move forward with you.

- The ability to draw well and become comfortable with your drawing skill requires a good deal of practice. It also requires some basic training in art. Taking some drawing classes in your school's art department's drawing classes will help. Keep a sketch journal with you, and draw something around you daily as your time allows. Over time, those practices will help you advance your perspective drawing skills.
- A sample class syllabus is included at the end of this book. It arranges this book's content with three suggested class projects in a semester framework (16 weeks of class time).
- A set of pre-made, scaled grid files in PDF format have been loaded on the publisher's website for this book's readers to use (www.routledge.com/978 0367860790). They aim to reduce the grid drawing time for those using the Grid Method. However, most theatre spaces are in various configurations and sizes. As the result, you will often find yourself needing to use the Grid Method modification skills discussed in this book to adjust those pre-made grids to match your particular need.

HAND DRAWING VS. COMPUTER APPLICATIONS

With today's fast-developing computer applications, many beginning designers start to wonder whether they need to make a choice between leaning hand drawing or to go with computer applications only on everything, including doing perspective drawing.

I love computer applications. In my own professional design practice, I always do my perspective drawing with pencils, first; scan it (digitize it) into a computer file; then, render over it with computer applications (mostly in Adobe Photoshop). Below are three such examples.

Example A:
SOUVERNIA, Max & Louie Productions, 2017

Example A, Perspective Sketch

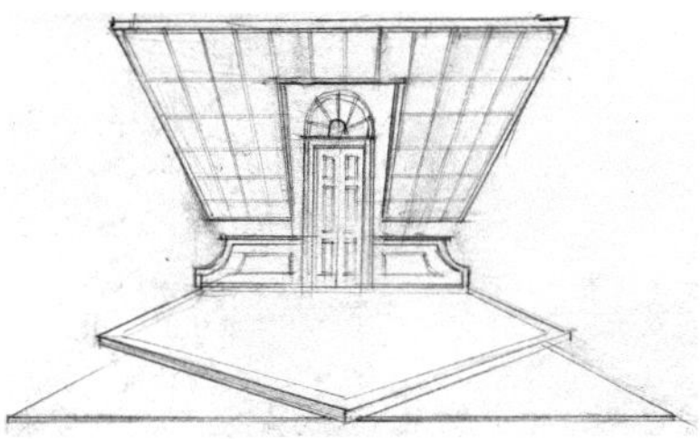

Example A, Colored Rendering

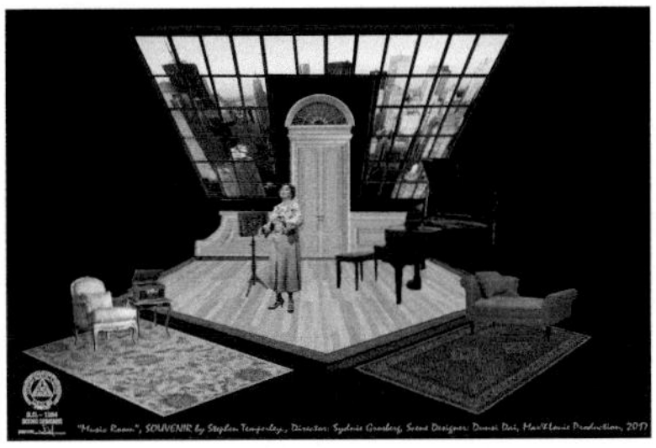

Example B:
OLD WICKED SONGS, New Jewish Theatre, 2016

Example B, Perspective Sketch

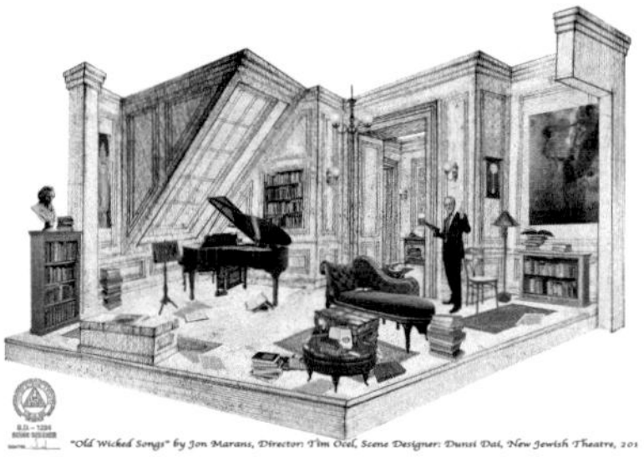

Example B, Colored Rendering

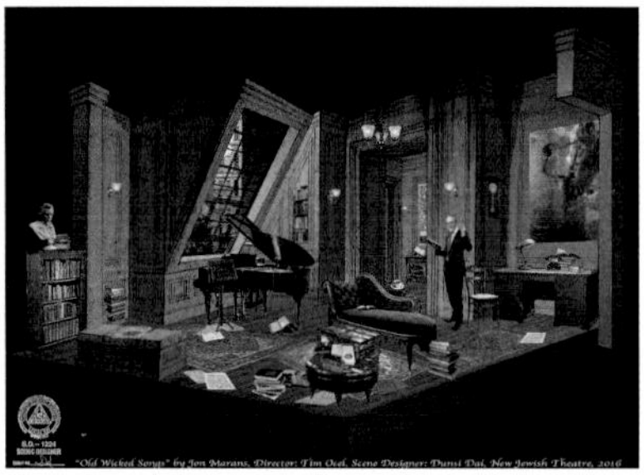

Example C:
PETER PAN, Variety Theatre, 2013

Example C, Perspective Sketch

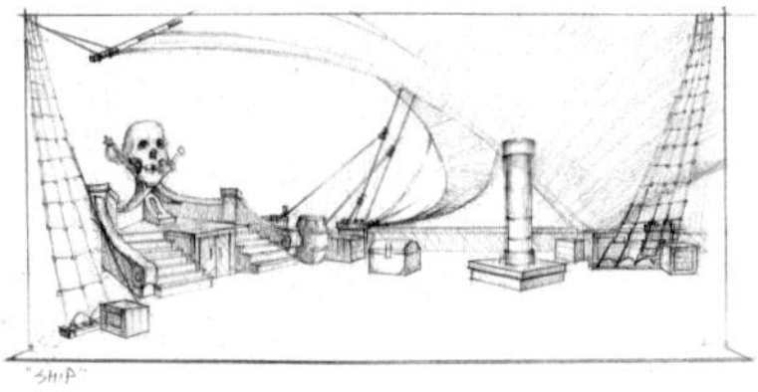

Example C, Colored Rendering

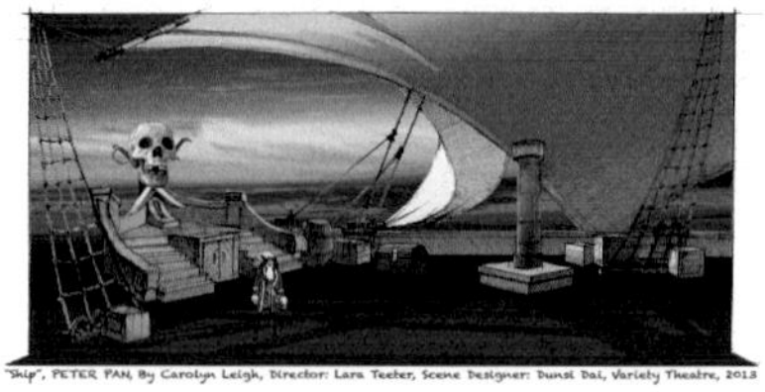

My design practice has convinced me that hand drawing is still the faster and more intuitive way for designers to develop their design ideas, exchange initial concepts with directors/producers, and make fast modifications/revisions during production meetings. Having good hand drawing skills in your tool box means you are on solid ground as a designer. Beautiful 3D-model rendering, such as those done with 3D Studio Max, could be great for final design presentation of a big-budget production. However, it will take considerably more time to produce. Your busy design schedule might not allow you time to proceed in that direction for most medium- and small-size productions. Some speedy 3D programs, such as Sketchup, can produce a perspective drawing fairly fast in simple shapes with stock image files. However, the users often encounter challenges when they try to create details in organic shapes. Do not let those shortcomings hold you back in your design creativity. To see this book's Photoshop set renderings in color, please log into the publisher's website at www.routledge.com/9780367860790.

ACKNOWLEDGMENTS

I would like to thank my daughter, Mona Dai, for her dedicated help in editing this book. I would like to thank Dick Brook, Michael Griggs, Michael Ganio, Rob Morgan, Haibo Yu, Shuxing Fan, and Huaixiang Tan. Without their help this book would not be possible. I also would like to thank Laura Hussey, Lucia Accorsi, Swati Hindwan, Laurie Fuller, Lauren Ellis, and Jonathon William Taylor for their tireless help in publishing this book.

CHAPTER 1

INTRODUCTION

Perspective drawing is an important communication tool for scene designers. Perspective drawing for theatrical scene design has some special features rooted in its basic function: communicating ideas between scene designers and other members of the production team such as the producer, the director, other designers, and the shops. For this purpose, a scene design perspective drawing needs to be clearly defined and in proportion with key details. You can develop your drawing skills so that you may communicate your ideas quickly and accurately. This gets your design concept across fast and allows you to modify it quickly during the production process.

For years, mechanical perspective drawing has dominated many theatre perspective drawing classes in colleges. While it is an effective method for accurate perspective drawings, it has a sharp learning curve for beginning designers. More importantly, it has a rather complicated procedure that tends to be very slow in drawing practice. Scene designers are required to work at a fast pace by nature of our work. We need to brainstorm ideas quickly, get these ideas to our production team on the run, and keep adjusting/refining design sketches in a continuous process. Thus, for scene designers, drawing fast is crucial.

The perspective drawing methods introduced in this book (the Grid Method, the Frame Method, and the Freehand with References Method) represent progressive approaches to perspective drawing. They are laid out sequentially in terms of challenges on drawing skill levels. This approach aims to help beginning designers to quickly start drawing and move forward progressively. These perspective drawing methods start with a low learning curves (the Grid Method), then encourages students to move onto the next skill level (the Frame Method then Freehand with References Method) when they are ready.

All three methods are related. They are designed to help designers grow their perspective drawing skill consistently on one path. You will see that many features of the Grid Method are also used in the Frame Method, and many features in the Frame Method are further developed in the Freehand with References Method. All three methods discussed in this book are in one perspective drawing family for different skill levels. You are not really learning three totally different methods; rather, you are learning how to draw perspective progressively in three skill-related stages.

Remember the following points as you proceed:

- Drawing in proportion is the key. Because scene designers are working in a tangible environment—a stage where the set is interactive with actors in real dimensions—whatever you draw will eventually establish a proportional relationship with the ultimate reference: the actor. In other words, you need to draw with the actor in mind as the basic proportional reference.
- Draw clearly (readability). This way, your production team (director, other designers, shop, etc.) can understand what you want to tell them in terms of how various objects of the set relate to one another.
- Relate your perspective drawing to your floor plan. This helps to bring your artistic dream into the physical specifics of the given production space—your set on a given stage.

CHAPTER 2

MATERIALS AND TOOLS

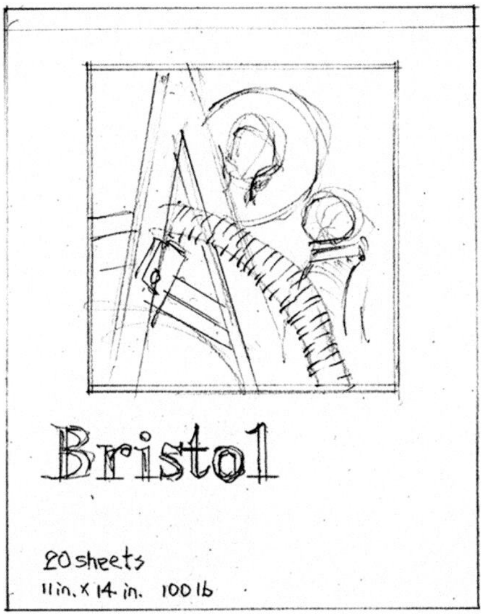

- Paper:

  You can draw on just about any paper for a perspective drawing (including your drafting vellum). For presentational quality, my favorite paper is 100-pound Bristol Board (in 11" x 14" size). Most of the example sketches shown in this book are done on this paper. This paper's surface is durable, erases well, and is strong enough to stand up by itself when in presentation. It is reasonably priced, especially if you buy it in pad size.

	• Vellum: This is the same vellum (or clear print) you used for your hand drafting project. It is transparent. It is handy to use, if you plan to use those pre-made grids, which are downloadable from the publisher's website (www.routledge.com/9780367860790). Just choose a pre-made grid PDF file and print it out (check "fit" in the printing window). Tape the printout down, then tape down a sheet of vellum over it. You are ready to draw with the Grid Method.
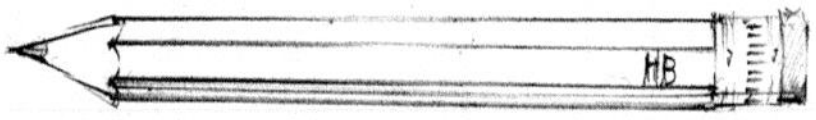	• Pencil: Regular #2 pencil is good enough in most cases. Pencils with various hardness and softness, such as 2H, 4H, and 2B, are optional and fun to play around with. For all of the example sketches shown in this book, I only used a regular #2 pencil, because that has been what I do with my freelance design projects.
	• Eraser Any good eraser will do. I recommend using 1-by-2-inch "pink erasers." These are the most common erasers on the market. They erase well, in large size, and with low cost, which encourages users to feel free cutting the erasers to obtain sharp edges to apply the erasing techniques introduced in this book.

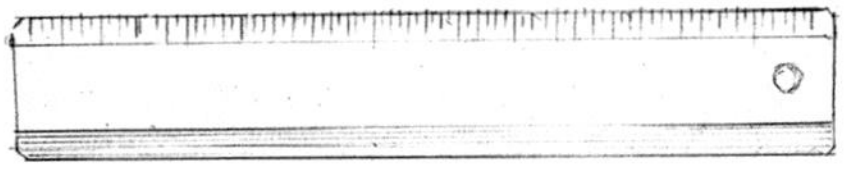 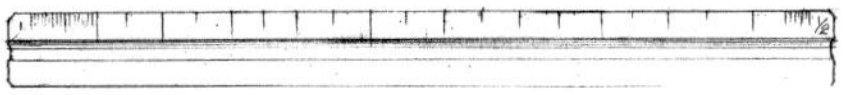	• Rulers: An architecture scale ruler (used to take measurements from floor plans, set up grids with the Grid Method, and set up the frame with the Frame Method). A 12-inch straight ruler for drawing lone straight lines. A small ruler around 4 inches is very convenient to use for drawing detail lines. It could be a small triangle, a straight ruler, or you might want to have both. Those will help you to draw most of the straight lines in your drawing when you need to clean up your work.
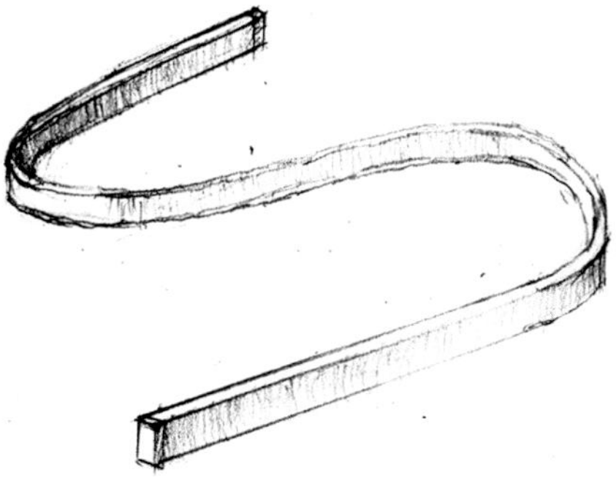	• Flexible Curve: This is a drafting tool that many scenic designers prefer to have. It helps you to draw smooth curve lines. However, it is not a must-have. You could opt not to use it. Personally, I do not use it much. In most cases, I draw curves freehand. On the positive side, this tool gives you more accuracy in curve drawing. Many of my students find having a flexible curve handy.
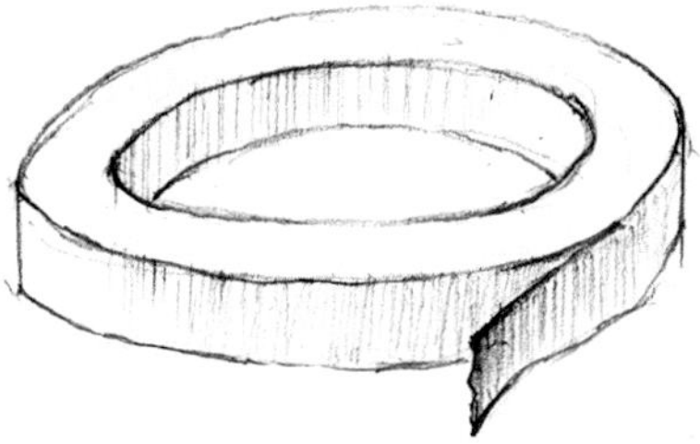	• Masking Tape (or Drafting Dot): This is another drafting material that is especially helpful when you are working with the Grid Method. It helps keep your drawing in place while you are setting up the grid and working out all of the perspective lines.

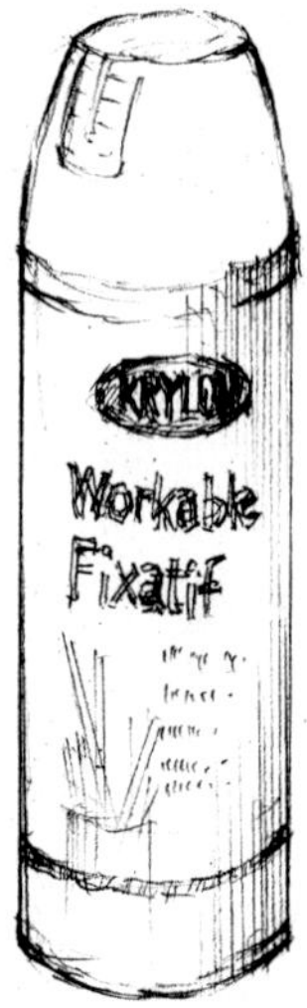	• Clear Latex Spray: I use Krylon Clear Matte Finish to seal my pencil sketches. 3M's product also works well. It is usually applied to the drawing after the show is over, when you want to archive your work and want to make sure your pencil drawing will not get smudged. At that point, you spray a coat of Clear Matte Finish Latex Spray over your drawing. Some people apply it right after their drawings are done. However, if you do so, it will make further changes to your drawing difficult.

CHAPTER 3

PERSPECTIVE BASICS

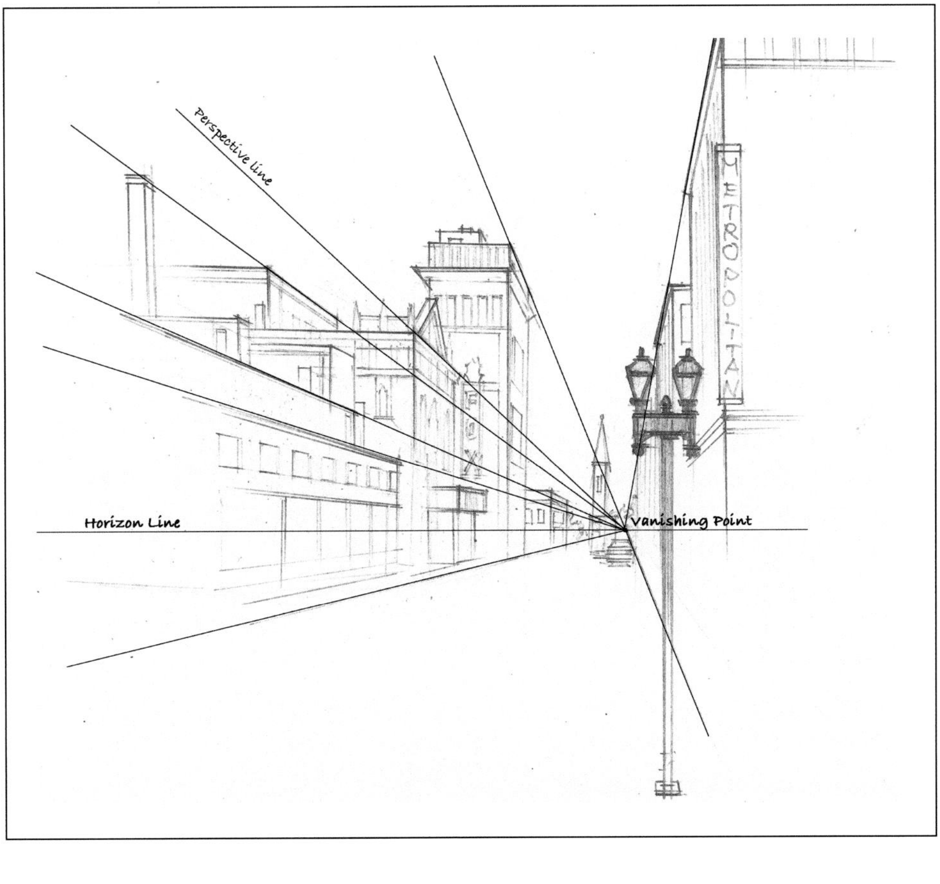

ELEMENTS OF PERSPECTIVE

1) A Fixed Viewing Position:

The point at which the viewer looks out toward the view.

For a given perspective view, the viewing position needs to be fixed. This is because when a viewer moves around, the viewing position changes with the viewer. Consequently, the perspective view will keep changing along with the viewer's movement, making it a headache to generate a reasonable perspective drawing. For scene designers, this viewing position usually is set at the center seat. Set your horizon line at the center of your side grid for the Grid Method. Set your horizon line at 3 feet from the theatre floor for the Frame Method.

2) A Picture Plane/Frame:

The chosen boundary of a perspective view (as in a camera view).

This is where you want your perspective drawing to stop in making a composition. Just imagine that you are viewing the set through a camera lens. For many designers and artists alike, when they draw from life, they can often be seen either "hand cropping" or holding up a small piece of cardboard with a square hole in it in search of a good composition. For scene designers, the stage proscenium is the logical choice of this viewing frame in a proscenium theatre. When you are working in a non-proscenium space (black box studio, etc.), the "frame" will set at a position of your choice, where you can illustrate (communicate) your design the best.

3) Horizon Line:

A horizontal line always crosses a perspective view at the viewer's eye level, where all vanishing points are located. The horizon line changes as the viewer changes his position in height.

This is a little confusing for many beginning designers: What? The horizon line can move? Yes, it's true. You can easily check this in any theatre with a raked seating arrangement. Look at your set from the front row of the seating area and find your horizon line. Then walk to the back row of the seating area, and look at your set again. Now, your horizon line will be raised. Or think of climbing a small hill. Notice where your horizon line is located in relation to the objects in your view when you are at the foot of the hill compared to where the horizon line is when you are at the top of the hill.

In short: the horizon line's position is at the viewer's eye level.

4) Vanishing Point:

Where perspective lines meet at the horizon line.

The number of vanishing points on the horizon line in a perspective view starts from one vanishing point perspective. However, the number can grow depending on how the objects are positioned/turned and where the horizon line is positioned. It is very important to remember that all of the vanishing points need to meet on your horizon line. This way, your perspective drawing will look consistent, no matter how objects are turned and scattered. The most commonly used perspectives types are one vanishing point perspective and two vanishing points perspective.

5) Perspective Line:

Perspective lines are angled lines formed along the edge of objects in a perspective view that lead to vanishing points on the horizon line.

Perspective lines are the most visible perspective element in a perspective view. However, they never work alone. It is important to remember that they are always heading toward vanishing points on a horizon line.

PRINCIPLES OF PERSPECTIVE

The relationship of the five basic perspective elements described above forms the basic principles of perspective.

All perspective elements work together: a viewer stays at a chosen spot to look through a picture pane (picture frame). The most important element in a given perspective view is the horizon line, which is set at the viewer's eye level. The horizon line's position changes as the viewer changes his position in height. All perspective lines meet on the horizon line where vanishing points are set.

For a given object, as it moves closer to you, it appears to grow larger in size and become more defined with details; as it moves away from you, it appears to shrink in size and becomes blurry.

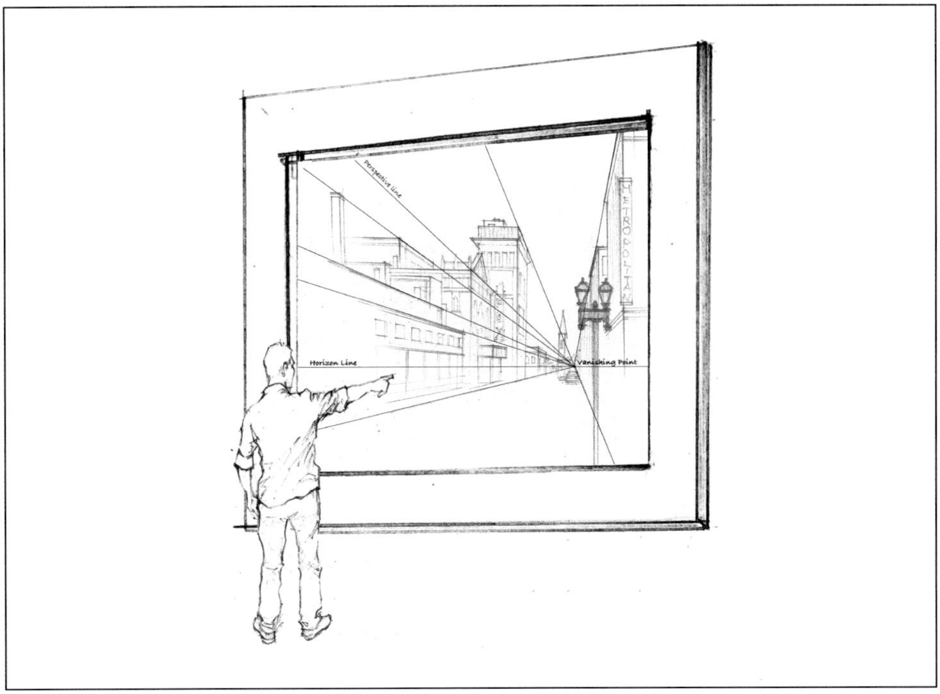

BASIC PERSPECTIVE TYPES

One Vanishing Point Perspective

Only one vanishing point is set on the horizon line; all perspective lines are heading toward it. Many theatrical sets, when they are positioned parallel to the proscenium (or your chosen picture pane), appear in one vanishing point perspective, especially those with symmetrical arrangements.

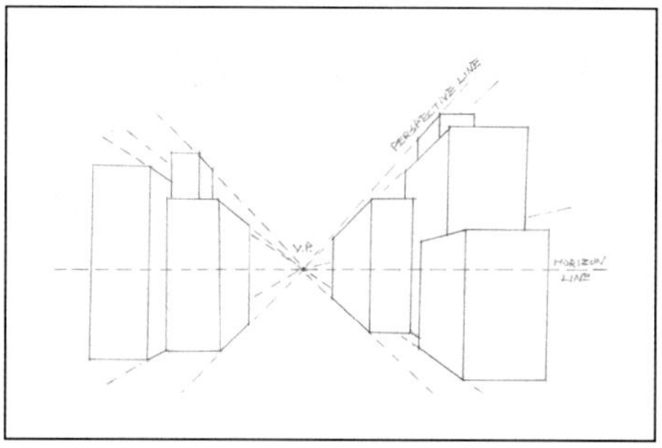

Example of a set sketch in one vanishing point perspective:
ON STRIVERS ROW, Stony Brook Theatre, 1994

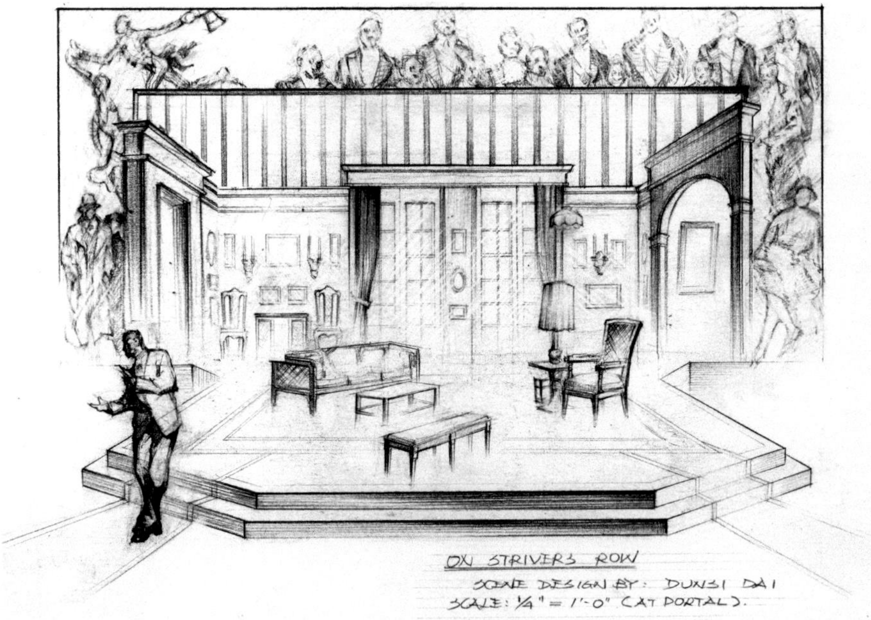

Two Vanishing Points Perspective

Having two vanishing points set on the horizon line.

When a set is positioned at an angle to the theatre's proscenium (or your chosen picture pane), it usually appears in two vanishing points perspective.

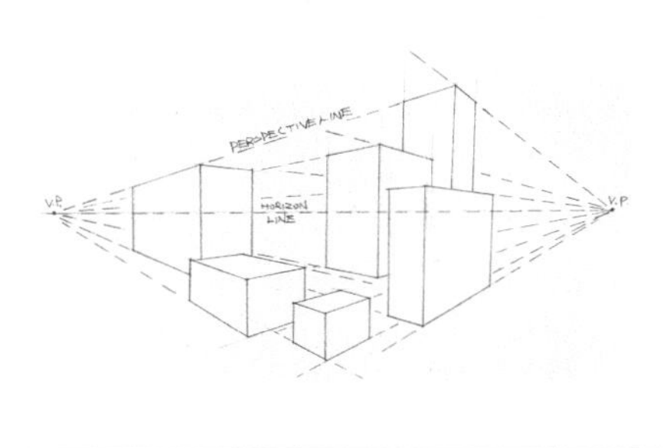

Example of a set design sketch in two vanishing points perspective:
SIGHT UNSEEN, New Jewish Theatre, 2015

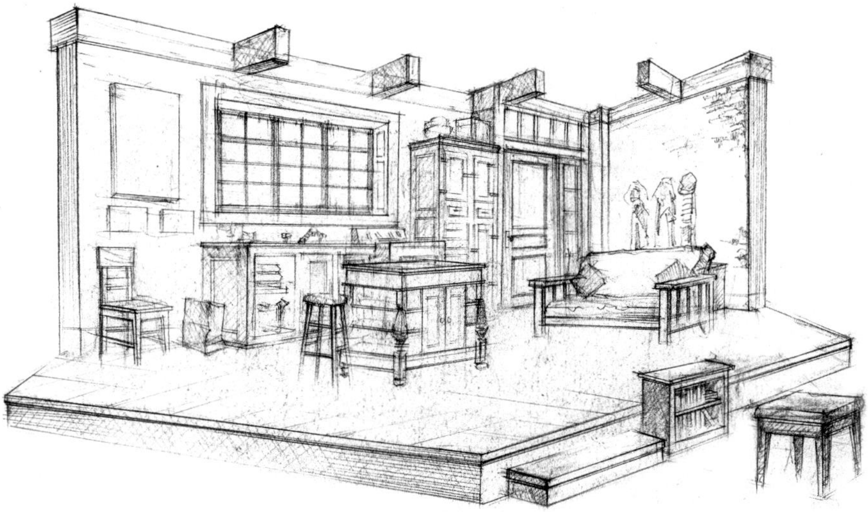

Three Vanishing Points Perspective

Three vanishing points perspective is mostly used in designs with false perspective scenery. Basically, it has a third vanishing point, which has been added to a two vanishing points perspective. The third one is a special vanishing point, which usually is positioned either above the horizon line, or below it. As the result, this third (special) vanishing point is not on the horizon line.

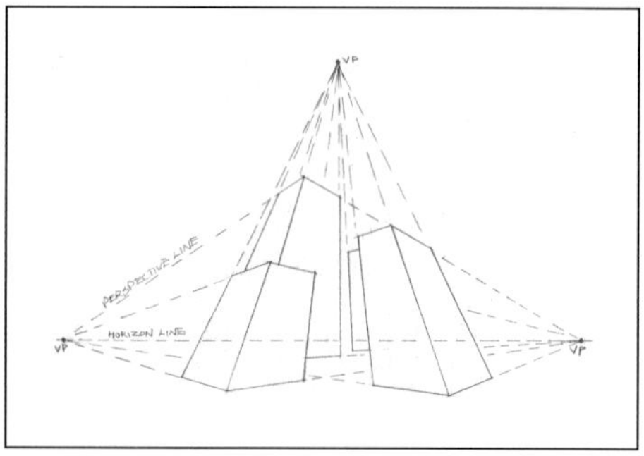

Example of a set design sketch in three vanishing points perspective: CINDERELLA, Houston Children Theatre Festival, 1994

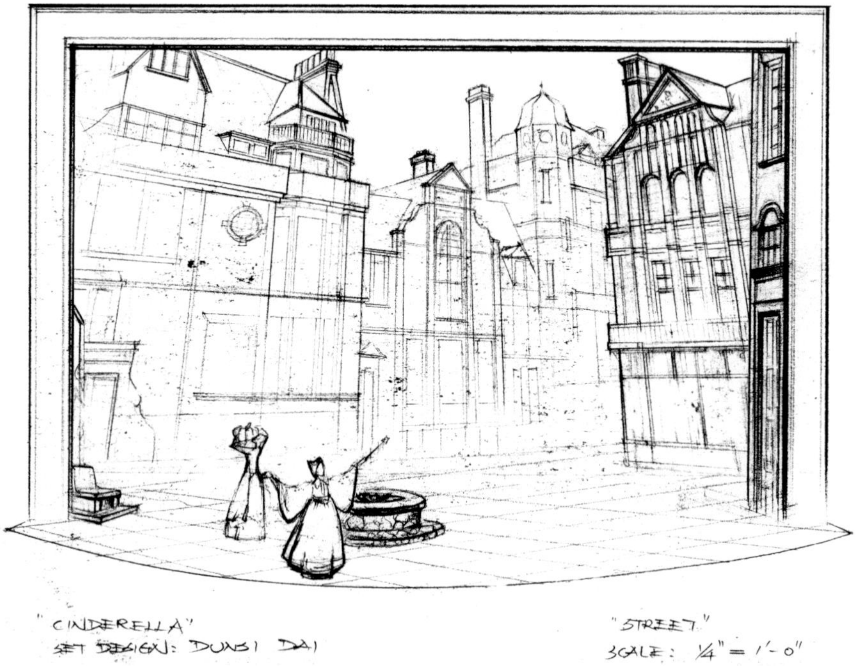

Multi-Vanishing Points Perspective

When a set has turned objects, which are at various angles to the proscenium and forming new angles to other set pieces, or, the set pieces are at different depth of the space and turned, we will see multi-vanishing points on the horizon line. This is also a common practice with a set involving false perspective design.

Example of a set sketch in multi-vanishing points perspective: TAMBOURINES TO GLORY, St. Louis Black Rep, 1997

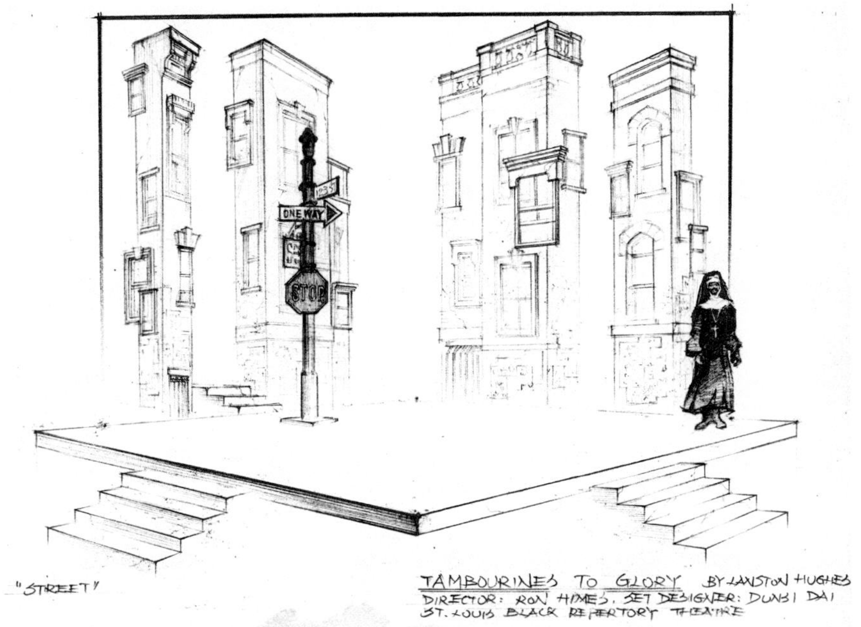

In this book, we focus on the two most common types of perspective: One Vanishing Point Perspective and Two Vanishing Points Perspective, since they are most often used for scene design in theatre.

CHAPTER 4

PERSPECTIVE DRAWING METHOD BASIC: CUBE SYSTEM

The cube system starts with a box-like three-dimensional geometric cube that has six sides and can be turned around in space. It is the foundation for all of the perspective drawing methods introduced in this book. "Generalizing" all objects in a drawing into basic "cube" shapes, no matter whether they are square-shaped desks, round-top tables, ball-shaped chandeliers, etc. In doing so, all perspective elements (i.e. perspective lines, vanishing points, horizon line, etc.) appear to be more "readable," "consistent," and "enhanced" in the drawing and become much easier for the drawer to grab. By working further on size and proportional references as well as perspective references with your cubes, you can draw just about anything in perspective and in proportion.

HOW THE CUBE SYSTEM WORKS

Examples of nine armchairs displayed at various perspective angles.

Step 1:

Draw nine cubes as shown below. Set both the horizon line and the vanishing point at the center.

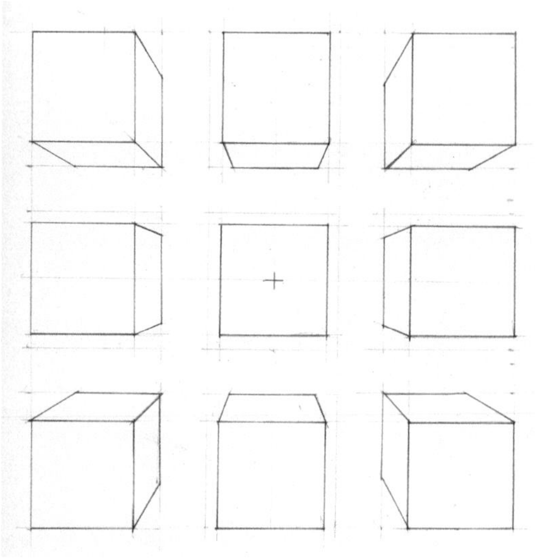

Step 2:

Using the cubes' perspective lines projected out of the vanishing point as references, rough in those armchairs' basic shapes in perspective.

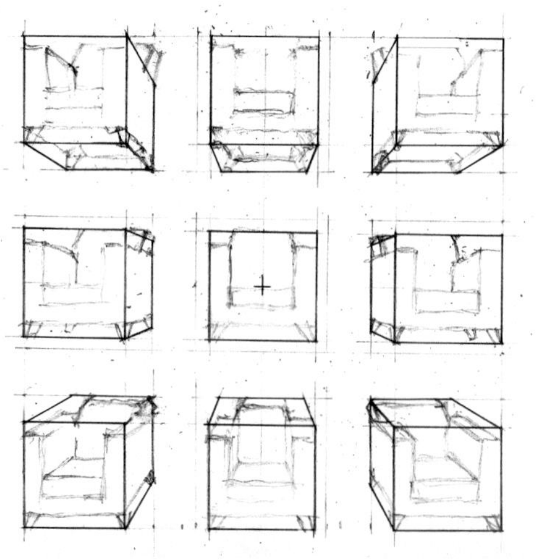

Step 3:
Finish those armchairs with details and add some shading to enhance the final look.

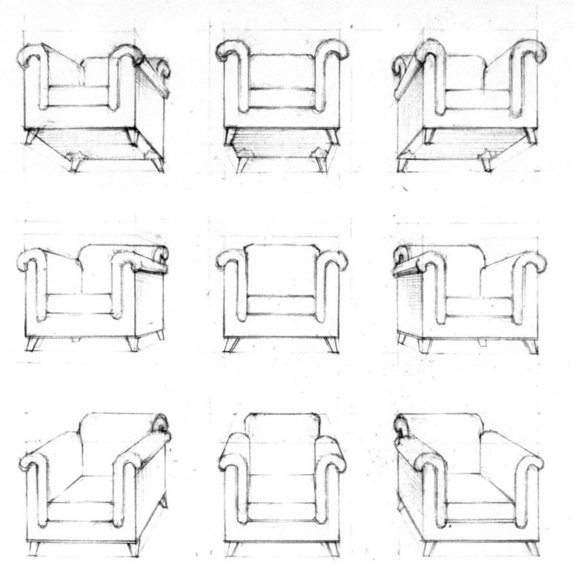

SPECIAL TOPICS WITH THE CUBE SYSTEM

Some beginning designers may find that certain objects present special challenges in working with the cube system. The most common such challenges prove to be staircases, round shapes, and irregular shapes. For those special topics, all of the above-discussed steps apply. Some of them might need additional steps to work out their special needs.

Staircase

- Step 1:

  Draw a cube to establish the staircase's perspective/proportion relationship (footprint and height).

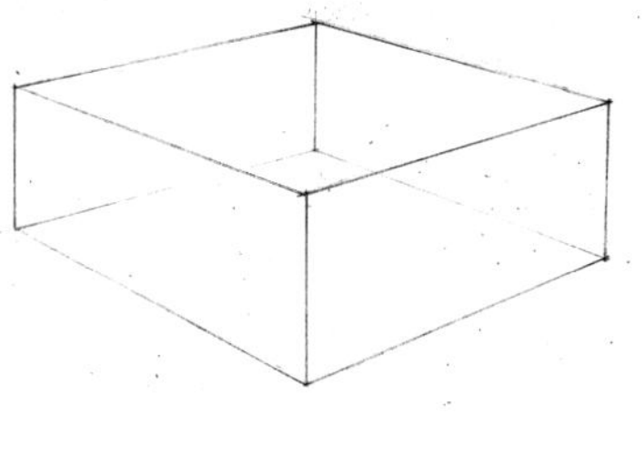

- Step 2:

  Draw a diagonal line on the cube's two sides. Rough in one side of the staircase along the diagonal line, then the other side. Pay attention to proportion and go along with the perspective angle established by the cube.

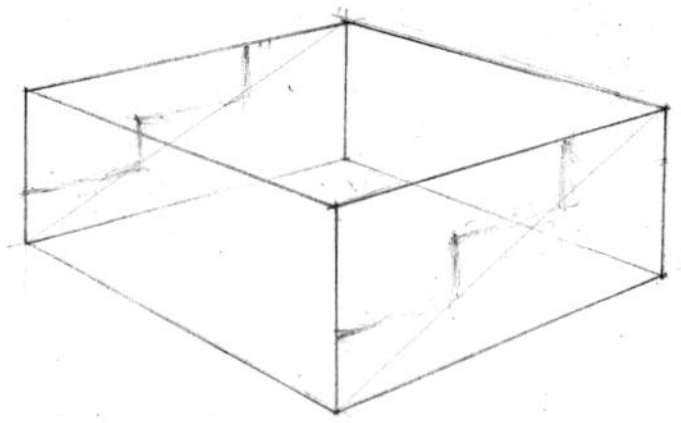

- Step 3:

  Connecting the two sides. Adjust the object's perspective with the cube's edges serving as perspective references (perspective lines). Enhance the drawing with shadows.

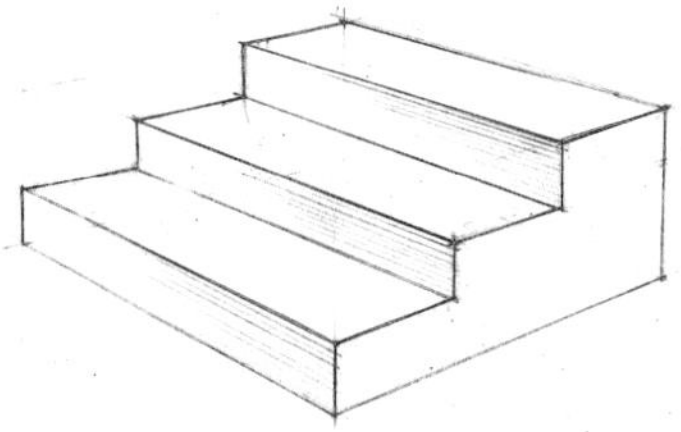

Round Top Table

- Step 1:

  Draw a cube referring to the chosen round table in proportion. Pay special attention to the table-top circle's size (diameter). This cube will set up this round-top table's perspective angles and basic proportion.

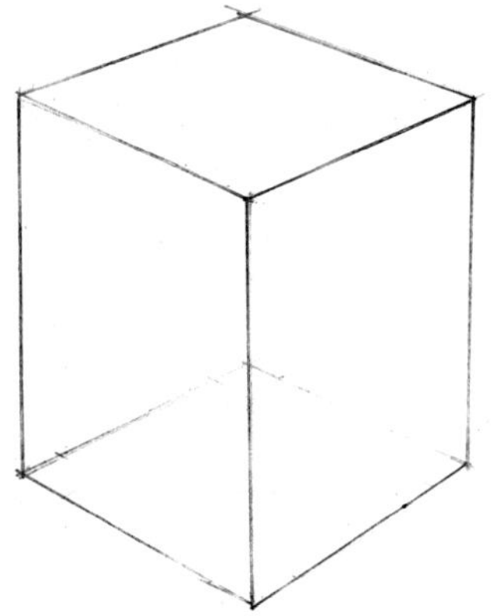

- Step 2:

  Fit the top circle into the cube's top side first to set it up in perspective view. Then, fit the base. Pay attention to their proportional relationship. Use the cube to adjust their perspective angles.

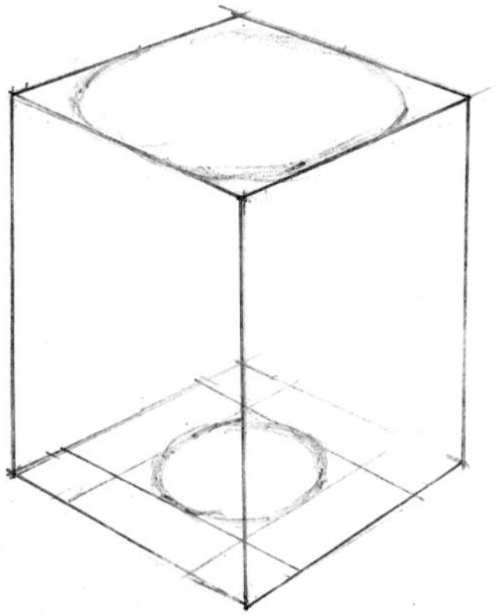

- Step 3:

  Add details and enhance the drawing with some shading.

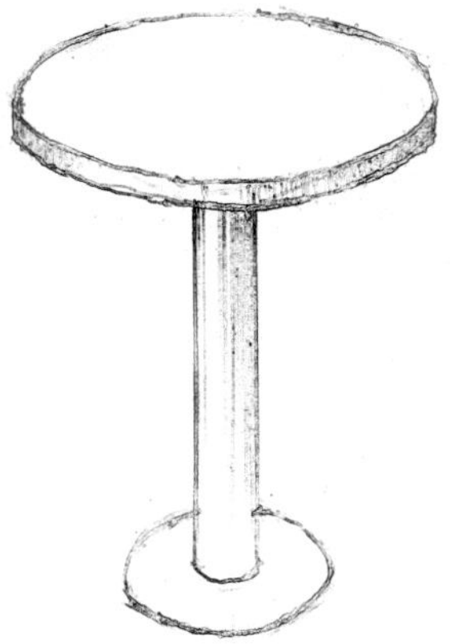

Objects with Irregular Shape

The cube system can be applied to most objects, including those with irregular shapes. In most cases, the principles of the cube system don't require much change. You just need to work creatively to make the system work for your specific needs. The following example of drawing a chaise illustrates the procedure.

A Chaise

- Step 1:

  Divide the object into a manageable number of cube units, making a cube for each unit. The smaller number of units you create, the easier they will be to manage. For this chaise, two cubes were drawn in proportion at the desired perspective angle.

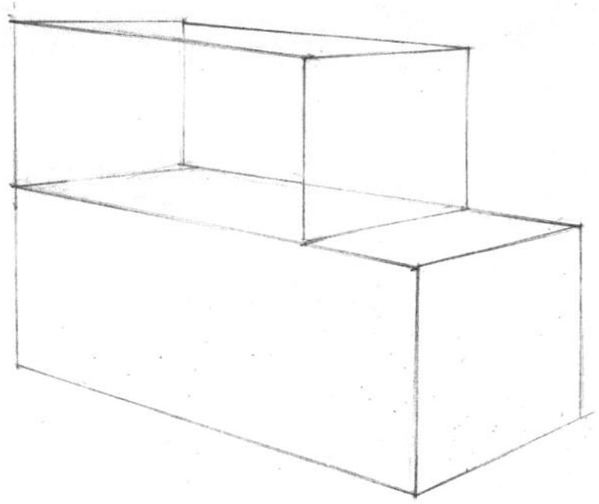

- Step 2:

  Rough in the chaise, with the cube's edges serving as perspective references (perspective lines).

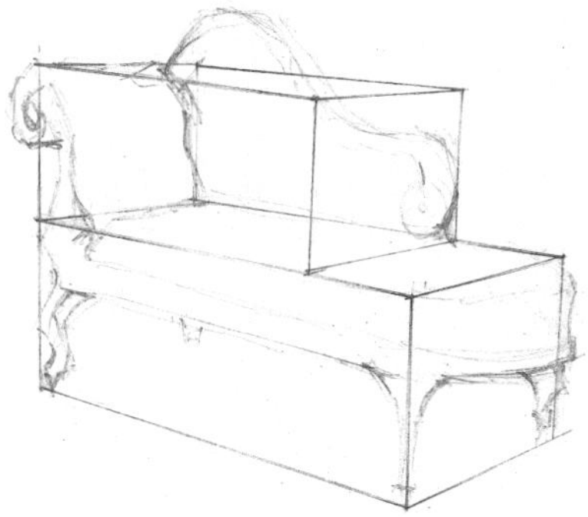

- Step 3:

  Add in details. Enhance the drawing with some shading.

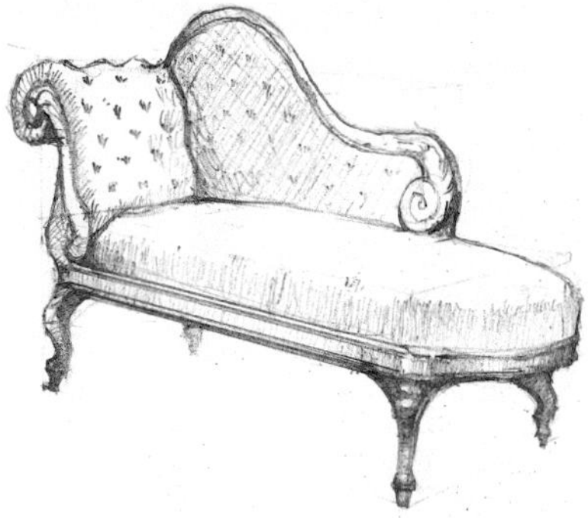

Tip: Learning how to draw scene design perspective sketches could be a fast and fun process. One important point you need to remember is that we are designers and artists by nature. We are not doing rocket science. What works the best for a designer in perspective drawing is to make it look good, in proportion, and relatively clear, and goes with common sense. All of the perspective drawing methods discussed in this book require you to "estimate" a lot. Pushing for extreme accuracy too much with these methods could lead to frustration. These methods were created for designers, not for engineers. Thus, a word of wisdom in mastering perspective drawing for scene design is to use these perspective drawing methods as guidelines. There is no need to limit yourself too much. Have some fun.

CHAPTER 5

PERSPECTIVE DRAWING METHOD 1: GRID METHOD

The Grid Method works with a measurable reference perspective grid. It gives the perspective drawing a relatively tangible ground to build up from. It starts by building up perspective "wall grids and floor grid" first, then fitting in scenic objects later. As the first perspective drawing method introduced in this book, the Grid Method is the easiest way to master perspective drawing for any beginning designer, with or without art training. It works well with either one vanishing point perspective or two vanishing points perspective.

WORKING WITH A ONE VANISHING POINT GRID

Set Up a One Vanishing Point Perspective Grid

- Step 1:

  Draw a 36' x 20' rectangle with your scale ruler, in 3/16" scale; draw a horizon line at the center position (at the 10' mark of the vertical position); and draw a center line at the center position (at the 18' mark of the horizontal position).

(It really could be in any scale of your choice, but 3/16" scale is easy to handle in regular paper size and large enough to put in adequate details later for most beginners. Other popular scales for grid making is 1/4".)

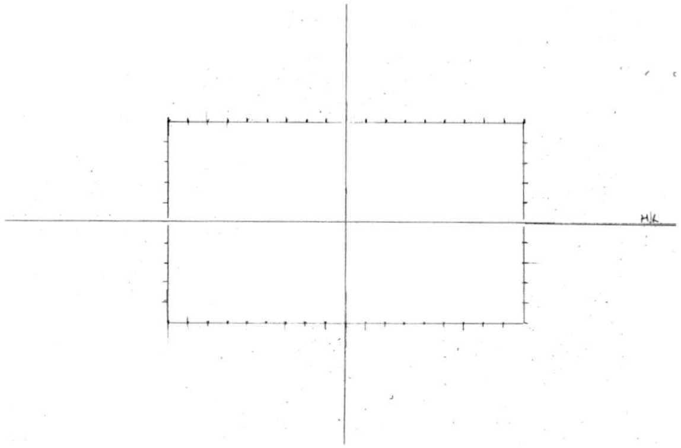

- Step 2:

  Mark the vanishing point at the center, and make marks at every 2' with your scale ruler at the rectangle's four borders. Then connect all the marks to form a grid.

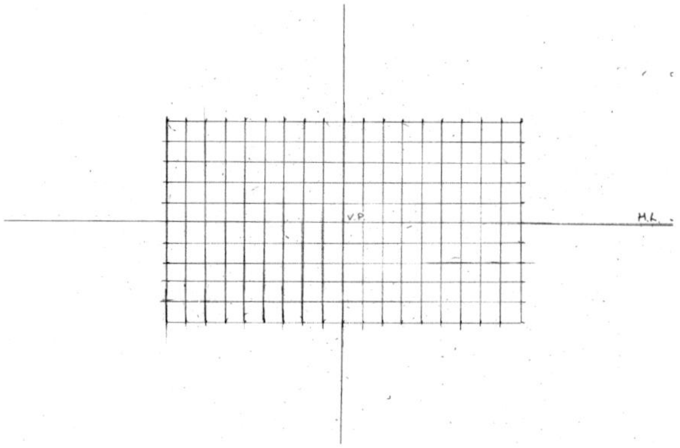

- Step 3:

  Draw a second rectangle off the first rectangle: Position this second rectangle at the position which will double the distance from the vanishing point to the edge of the first square. (On the vertical center line, this is at 20'. On the horizon line, this is at 36'.) Then, connect the two rectangles' corners.

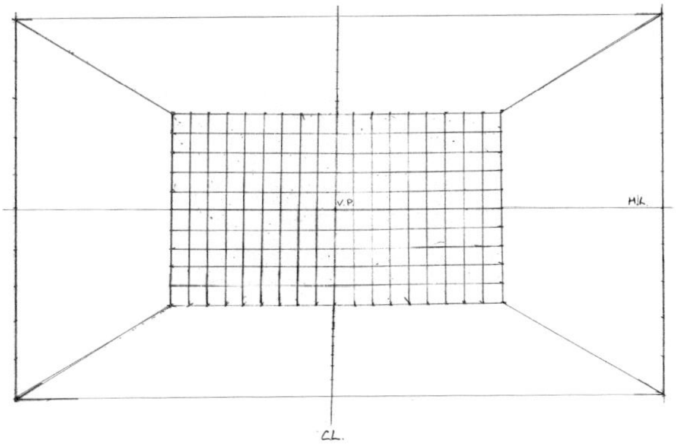

- Step 4:

  Use a ruler to project perspective lines from the vanishing point through the marks on the first rectangle's borders. Because there are always fewer details to draw in the ceiling area, draw projected line at every 4' works fine (also projected out from the vanishing point).

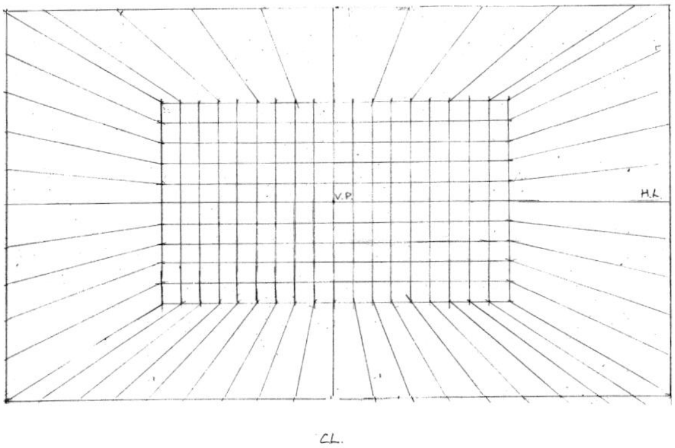

- Step 5:

  Draw a diagonal line from corner to corner on the two side areas between the first rectangle and the second one. Mark the crossing points of the diagonal lines and the projected lines. Then, draw vertical lines at every crossing point. After finishing with the two side grids, connect both side grids' bottom crossing points, and project perspective lines from the vanishing point through the first rectangle's bottom and top grid points. This will set up a perspective grid in one vanishing point perspective.

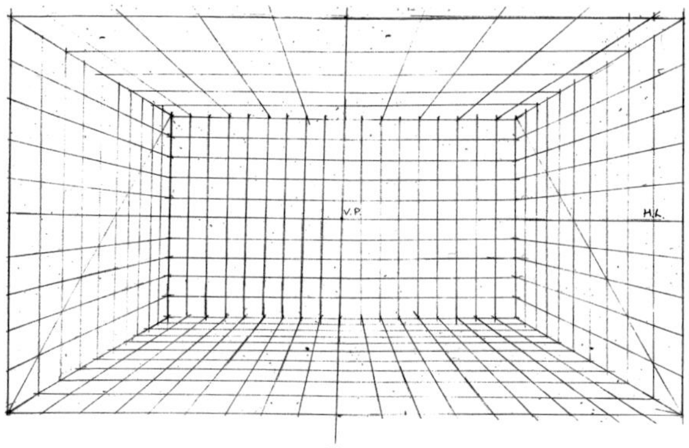

Note:
36' x 20' is the most common proscenium size. You can modify it with the real proscenium size of the space you are working in, after you finish this setup.

Draw a Perspective Sketch Based on the Grid

Everything you draw needs to be based on a scaled floor plan, which needs to have a grid matching the perspective grid. Make sure the number of squares on the grid you created on your perspective grid matches the number of squares on your gridded floor plan.

Only the back grid of this perspective grid is measureable with your scale ruler. All the other areas are in perspective. Their measurements can be estimated by counting the number of squares on the grid, but not measureable with a scale ruler directly.

The perspective grid is your helper both in perspective angles as well as for estimating measurements in perspective. Each square on the grid stands for a measurement unit you assigned to it. In our example's case, the size of each square on the grid represents 2' (thus, half of a square is 1').

You need to count the number of squares on the perspective grid to estimate an object's measurement, and use the squares' angles as your perspective angle reference.

We use an example on the next page to illustrate this procedure.

- Step 1:

  Draft a scaled floor plan of the set you are going to do a perspective sketch for. It needs to have the same number of squares on the grid as the perspective grid you are preparing. In our example, 1 square in the grid = 2'.

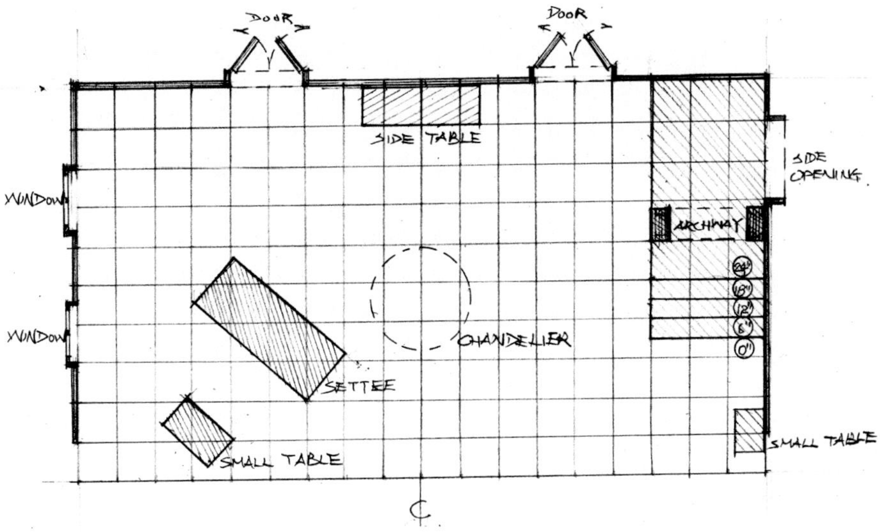

- Step 2:

  Counting the walls' grid positions on the gridded floor plan, lay the walls into the perspective grid.

  Related set information for this example:

  - The back wall is at 36' wide × 16' high.
  - The side walls are at 18' wide × 16' high.
  - The doors are at 4' wide × 10' high.
  - The two windows are at 3' wide x 8' high (window is 3' to the ground).

  Procedure:

  - Lay the walls into the perspective grid by counting their positions on the gridded floor plan.
  - Lay the doors into the perspective grid by counting their positions on the gridded floorplan. Find their 4'-wide footprint positions, mark them on the perspective grid. Count the side grid to mark the door's 10'-high position, and put them in.
  - Lay the windows into the perspective grid by counting their position on the gridded floor plan, and mark the 3'-wide windows on the perspective grid.

Count the side grid to get the windows' 3'-high position from the ground, then continue counting another 8' to mark the tops of the windows.

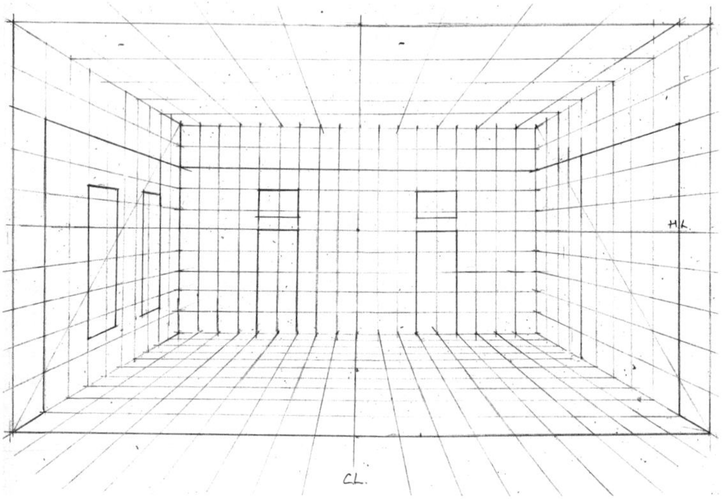

- Step 3:

  Lay in the stage left archway (draw object off the walls):

  - Count the archway's position on the gridded floor plan, then lay it into the perspective grid. (Related information: the archway is 16' high x 6' wide x 2' deep. Its opening is 3'–6" wide and 14' high.)

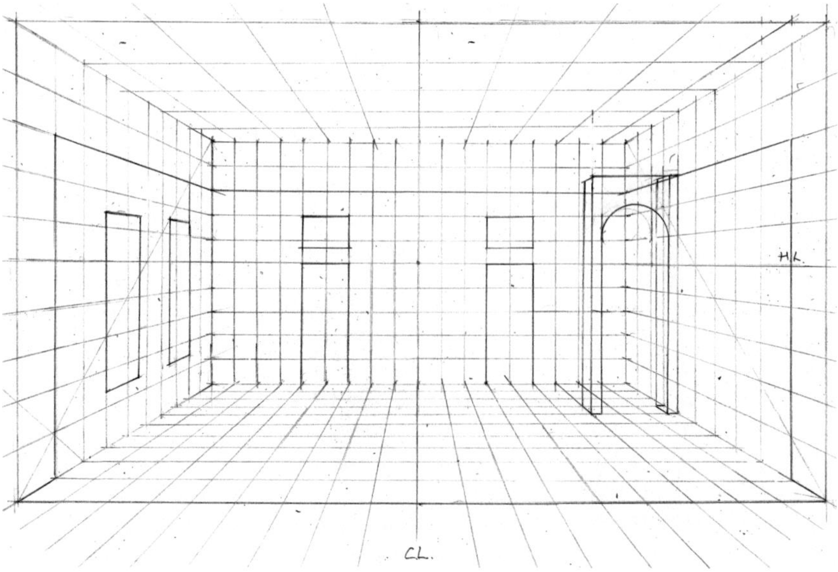

- Step 4:

  Lay in the upstage left platform and the steps; then, put in furniture cubes.

  - Count the gridded floor plan for their foot print positions. (The steps are with 6" raiser and 1' tread. The platform is at 2' high and 6' wide.) Lay them into the perspective grid: use the stage left grid to position each step, then extend the step lines to the center stage direction to meet their 6'-wide position on the floor grid.
  - Count the furniture pieces' positions on the gridded floor plan, then, lay then in as "cubes" in the perspective grid, in terms of position, size, and basic perspective angles.

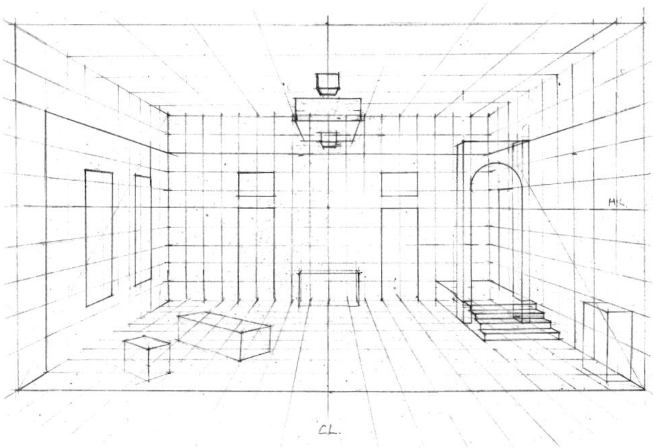

- Step 5:

  Carve details out of those "cubes" to reveal their features. Add in set details and set dressing pieces. Erase the perspective grid and clean up the drawing for clarity. Add some shading to clarify shapes and enhance the look of your drawing.

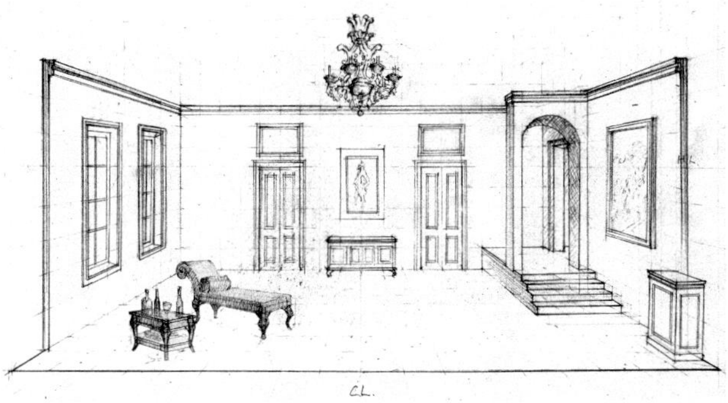

Tip: Each square on the grid stands for a size you assigned to it in Step 1 (here, it is set at 2'). The only portion you could use your scale ruler to take measurement directly is at the first rectangle (the back wall). All other parts of the drawing cannot be measured with a scale ruler directly, because they are in perspective. The suggested way to "measure/estimate" anything in this perspective drawing is to count the object's position and its corresponding reading on the perspective grid in terms of the numbers of squares.

Modifying a One Vanishing Point Grid

In order to use the Grid Method effectively, you will need to modify your grid to make it match your drawing's needs in a given space. This is especially true if you are planning to use those pre-made perspective grid PDF files downloaded from the publisher's website.

Add Extensions to the Grid

Draw a diagonal line (corner to corner) in two squares in at the side of the perspective grid where you want to add an extension and project the diagonal line out. Then, project all perspective lines at that side out. Draw vertical lines at those newly formed crossing points where the new diagonal line meets those extended perspective lines.

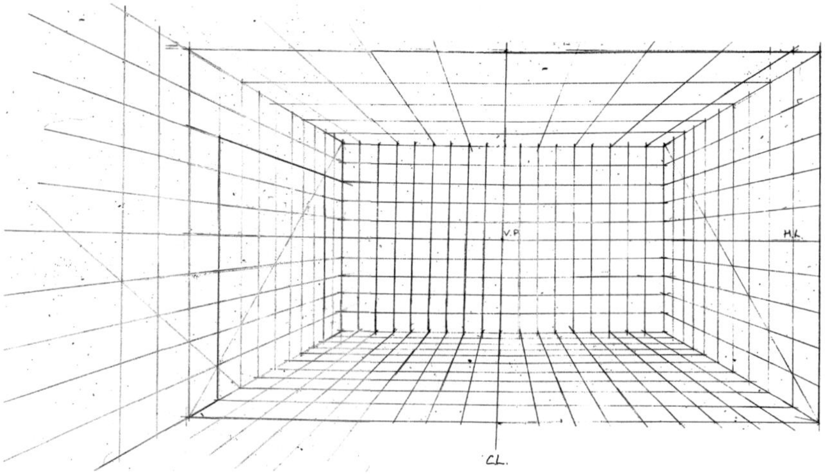

Resize the Grid

Option A: Making a Smaller Grid from a Standard Pre-Made Grid

The following example demonstrates how to modify a pre-made one vanishing point perspective grid for a grid smaller than our standard 36' x 20' proscenium opening. Our example is to modify a 30' x 16' smaller grid out of our standard 36' x 20' pre-made grid.

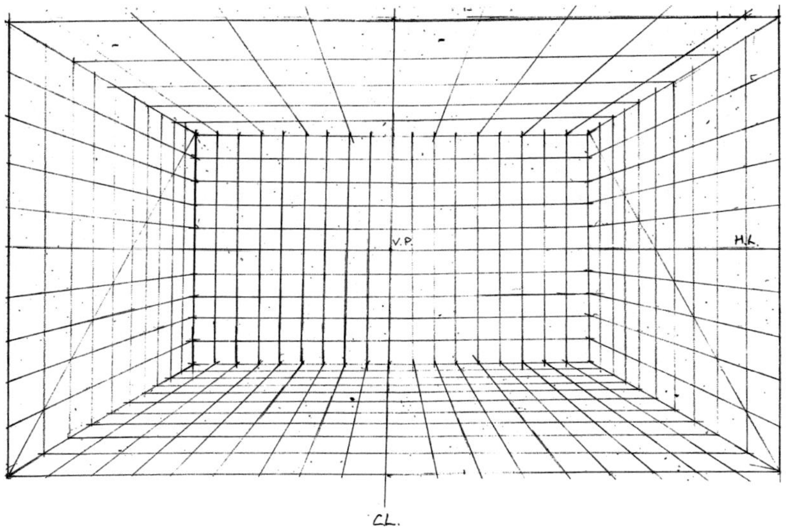

- Step 1:
  - On the standard pre-made grid, erase (white out) 6' of the grid (three squares) from the stage left side. Connect the top grid and the bottom grid at the far stage-left side with a vertical line.

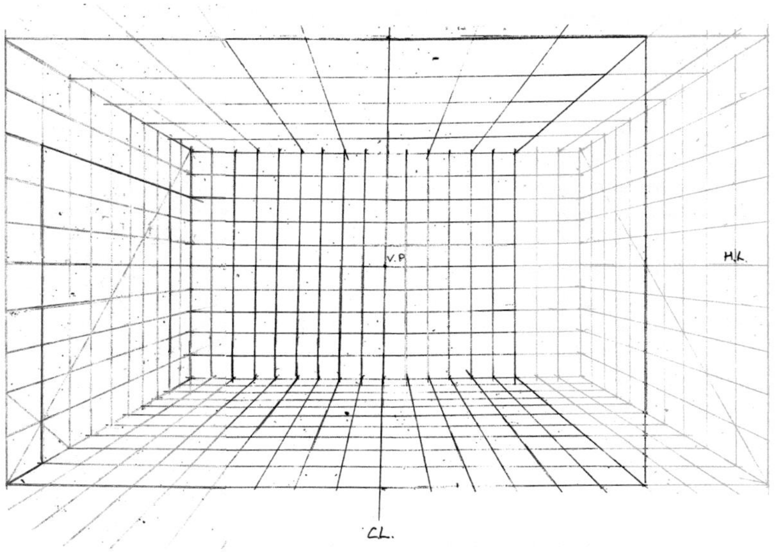

- Step 2:
  - Project new perspective lines from the vanishing point out through the first rectangle's crossing points at its modified left side.

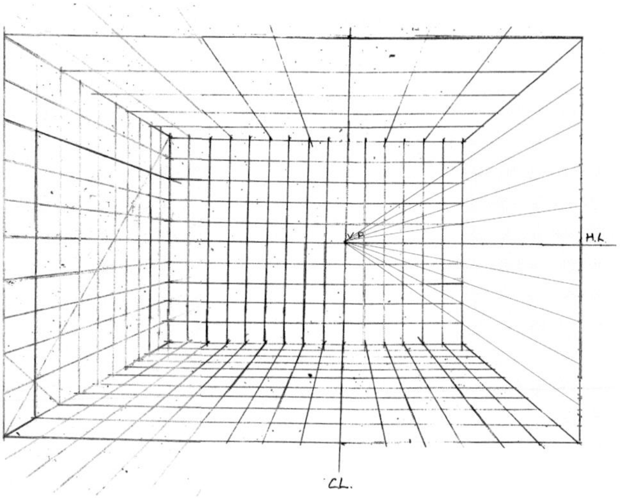

- Step 3:
  - Draw a corner to corner diagonal line at the newly formed side area (or use the grid points on the existing floor grid) to set up vertical lines for the new side grid at the newly established stage-left side.

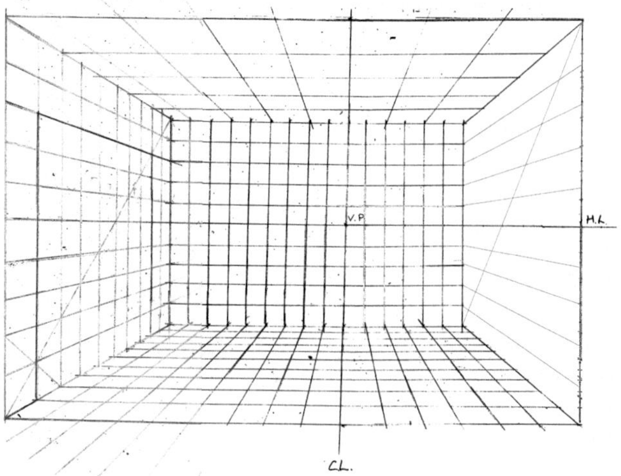

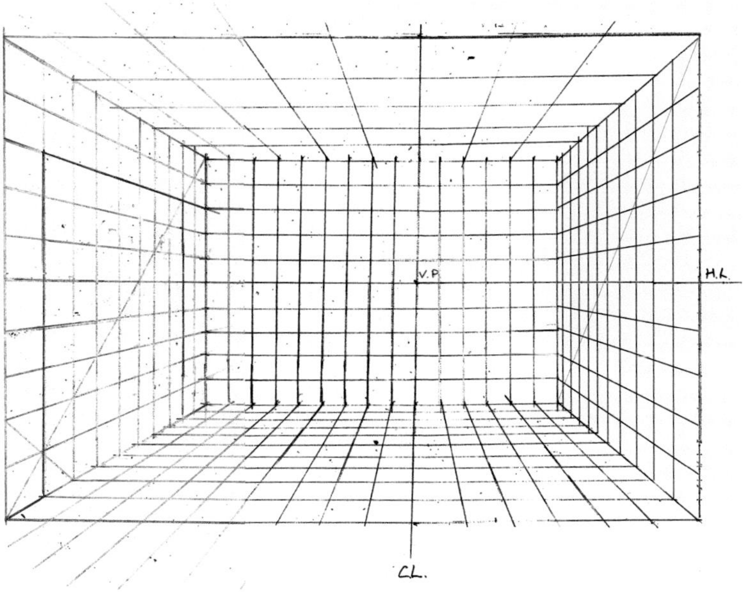

- Step 4:

  Erase (white out) 4' (two grid units) from the top of the existing grid.

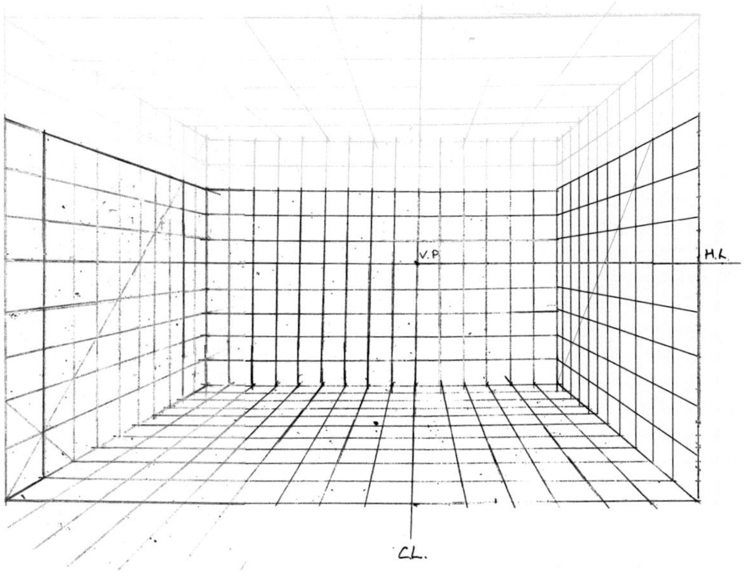

- Step 5:

  Connect the two side grid panels. (You can do it with 4' grid size at the top, since fewer details are expected at the top area.)

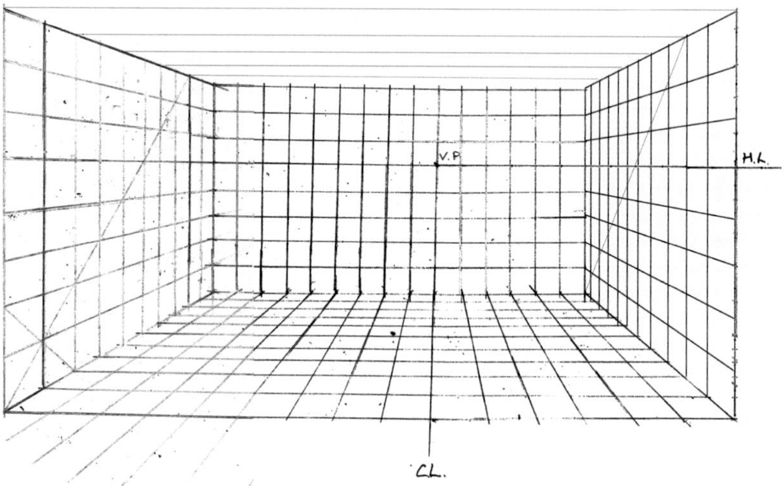

- Step 6:

  Project new perspective lines from the vanishing point, crossing points at the top of the back grid to finish the new top grid (4' grid is common for the top area).

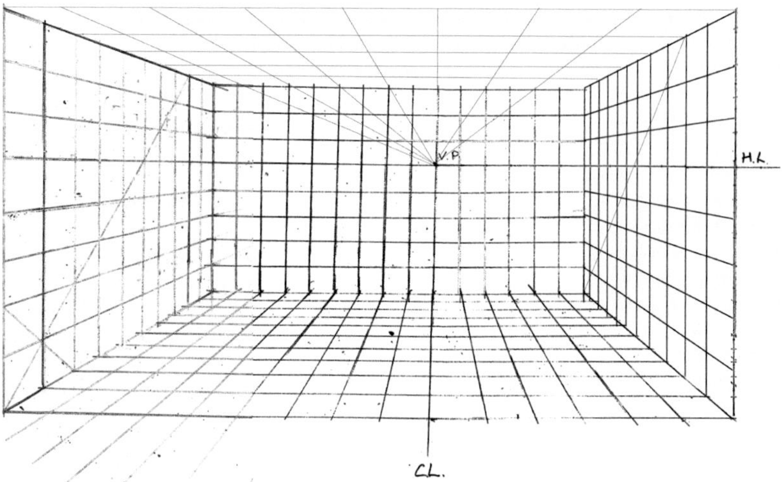

- Step 7:

  Clean up. You have a new one vanishing point perspective grid of 30' x 16'.

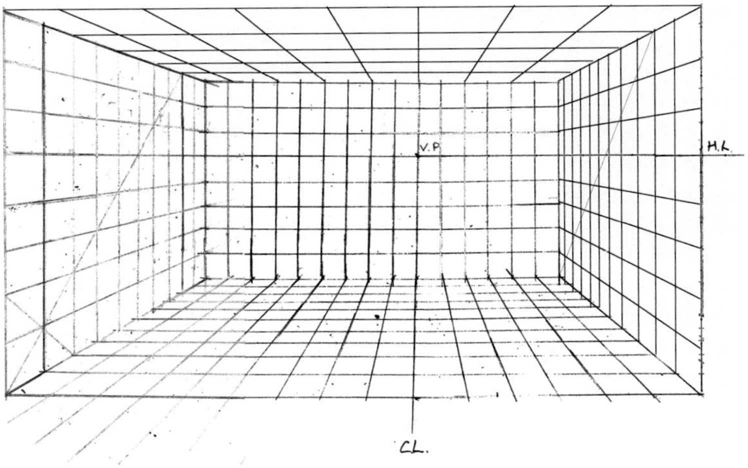

Tip: No need to worry if the vanishing point is not at the center. Just assuming your viewer has changed his seat to a new off center location. The key is to keep the new viewing position consistent in your drawing.

Option B: Making a Large-Sized Grid from a Standard Size Pre-Made Grid

This is a procedure to reassign the square's unit size on the perspective grid (how much each square stands for), then modify it. We start with our standard 36' x 20' grid and change it to a 56' x 20' grid.

- Step 1:

  Re-assign each square on the grid to 3' (a change from the original size of 2' each). No physical drawing change is needed at this step. Now the total size of this grid stands for 54' x 30'.

- Step 2:

  Apply the steps from Option A to resize this grid to your desired size (larger than 56' x 20').

Tip: You can do this to resize those pre-made grids to any size you need because you have an established perspective relationship set up in those pre-made grids. Subtracting/extending part of the grid from its edges will not alter the perspective set up, as long as you keep the vanishing point position unchanged.

Use a Pre-Made Grid File to Work Out a One Vanishing Point Grid in Non-Proscenium Spaces

Other than traditional proscenium theatres, many theatrical productions are done in non-proscenium theatres, such as black-box studio theatre, thrust stage theatre, etc. The grid method can be used in those non-proscenium theatres as well. The difference is that, now, the stage frame position could be placed where you decide it needs to be. Below, we use a produced scene design to illustrate this procedure, step by step.

ON STRIVER'S ROW, Stony Brook Theatre, 1994

This set is on a thrust stage configuration in a black-box theatre. Although we are not working on a proscenium stage any more, the basic drawing procedure stays the same. The important variation is, now, we need to choose and set a base point to set up our grid. With this project, my choice was at the painted portal.

With this example, a pre-made one vanishing point grid PDF file is downloaded from the publisher's website (www.routledge.com/9780367860790) to demonstrate how to modify a pre-made perspective grid into a desired stage size, and how to put a perspective drawing over this pre-made grid.

It is highly recommended to start your procedure with a Floor Plan:

The floor plan below shows the entire black box theatre with the set in the staging area, as well as the seating arrangement. As a result, you have a full view of the entire theatre.

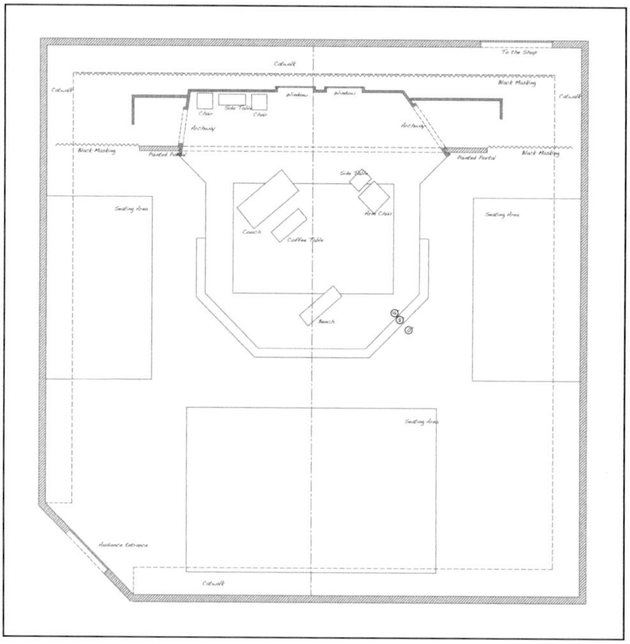

- Step 1:

  Draw a grid on the floor plan in which each square on the grid represents 2'. It is fairly easy and quick to do it with a CAD program. With your scale ruler, you can also easily draw such a grid over your floor plan by hand as well. The floor plan below mostly shows the stage area only so that details of the set can be seen more clearly.

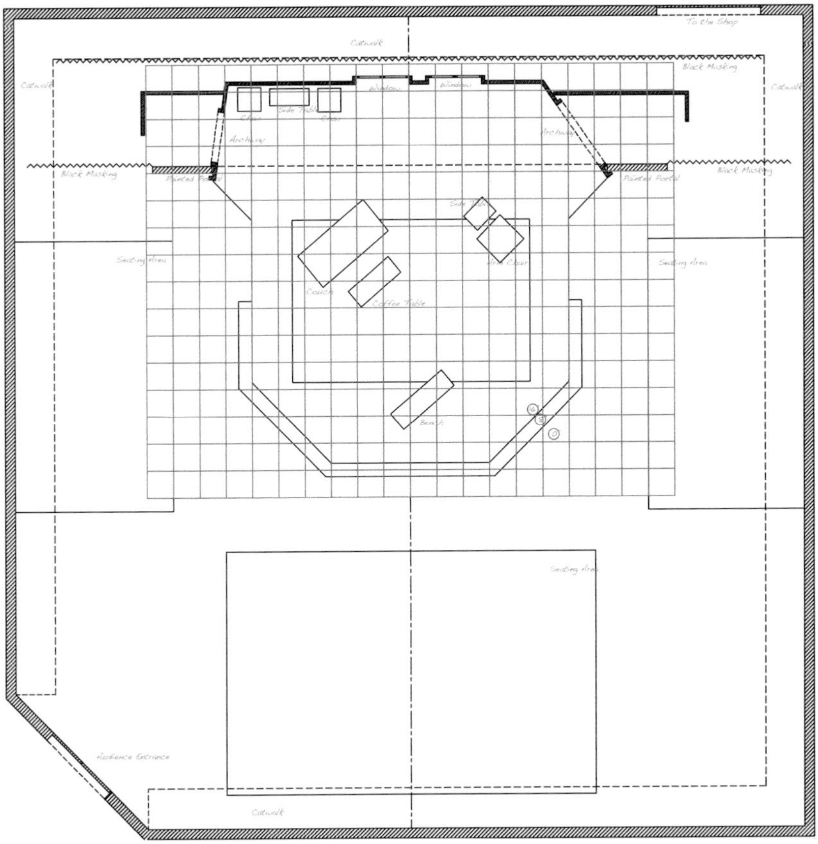

- Step 2:

  Download and print out a pre-made one vanishing point perspective grid from the publisher's website (www.routledge.com/9780367860790) at 100%, make it "fit" to your paper in the printing window. Put a sheet of vellum over it and use masking tape to tape the pre-made grid and the vellum together at the top. Count the squares on the gridded floor plan to locate the trust stage's basic layout positions, the painted portal and the back wall position. Draw their footprints into the perspective grid (on the vellum).

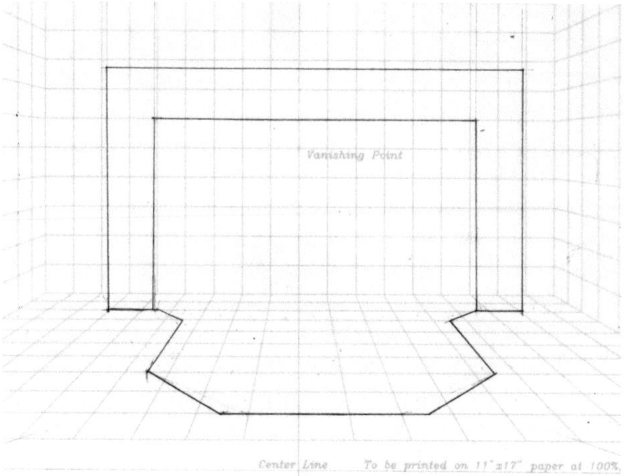

- Step 3:

  Count the squares on the gridded floor plan to locate each major set piece's position, then draw their footprints first, then their shapes on the vellum.

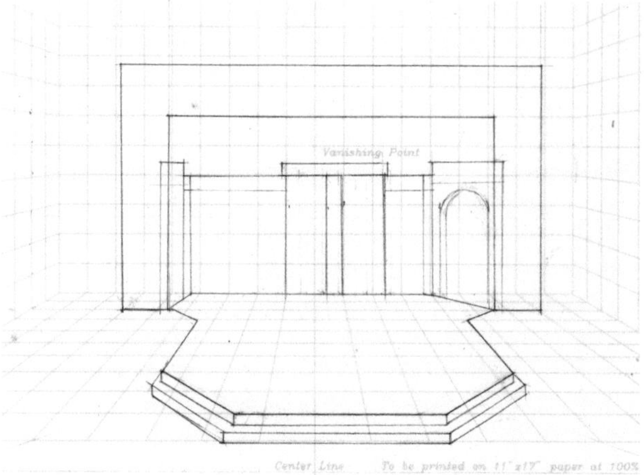

- Step 4:

  Count the squares on the floor plan grid to locate the furniture pieces' size and positions and draw them as cubes on the vellum.

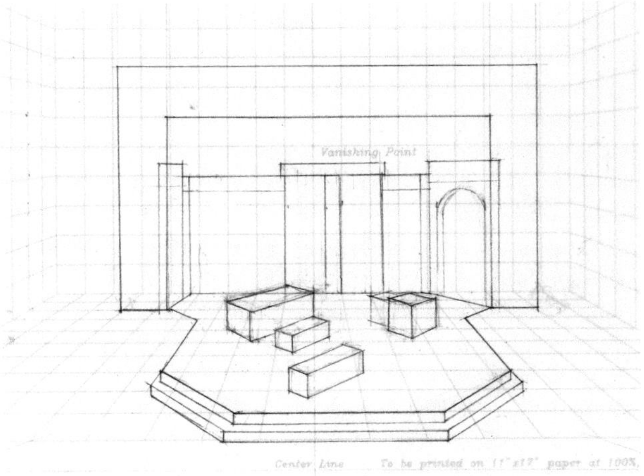

- Step 5:

  Using the perspective grid as reference, put in details, and add shading to finish the sketch.

Note: Steps 1–4 are based on a pre-made grid with the horizon line at the center. Step 5 is a finished sketch pulled from one of my early design works in which the horizon line is about 2' lower).

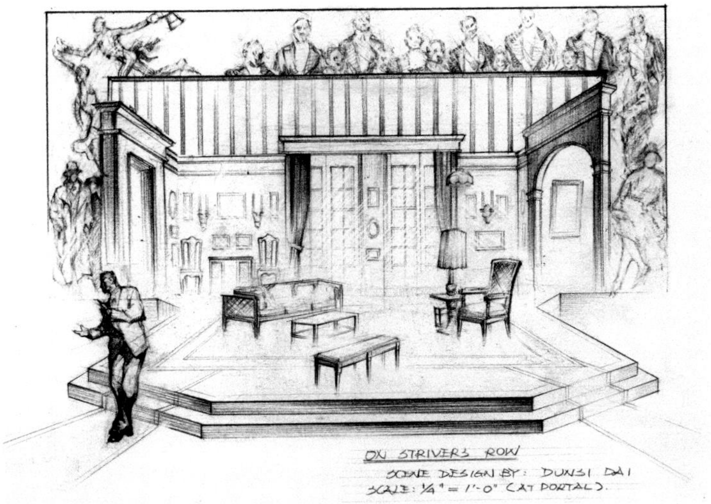

WORKING WITH A TWO VANISHING POINTS GRID

Set Up the Grid

- Step 1:

  Draw a 16' vertical line at the center of your paper in 1/4" scale. Make marks every 2' on this line. Draw a horizon line at the center of this vertical line. This horizon line should be at two times of the center vertical line in length at both sides, with a total length equal to four times of the center vertical line. In our example's case, it is 32' in 1/4" scale at each side (64' for the total length). Then mark your two vanishing points at both ends of the horizon line.

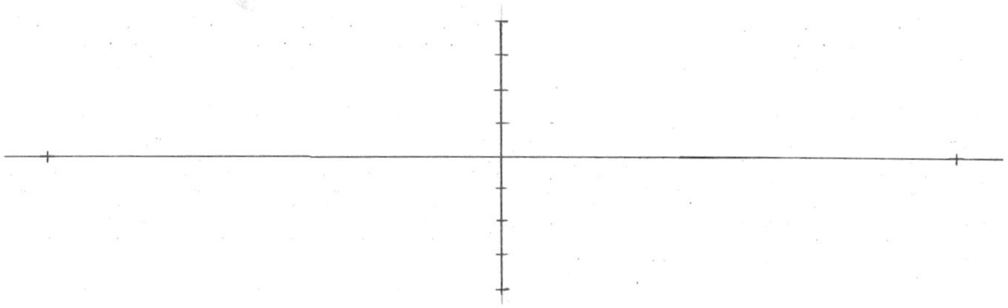

Tip 1: This is the two times factor. If you go less than two times factor on this, your drawing's perspective will look more like a "forced perspective."

Tip 2: In doing this, you do not need to draw everything on a really big piece of paper. You can do this on a drafting table. Use masking tape to tape down a piece of Bristol board (or any white paper) large enough for your drawing space (11" x 14" for this project) and center it. Then, put up a drafting dot (or a piece of masking tape) at the vanishing point position at each side of the extended horizon line and make a cross mark at each drafting dot to be used as the vanishing points to set up the grid.

- Step 2:

  Connect one vanishing point with every mark on the center vertical line, then project them out. Those are your grid's perspective lines (at the projected lines' side). It is important to keep in mind: we only use those perspective lines at the other side of the center vertical line from the vanishing point which you are working from.

  Draw a second vertical line at the position equal to 1.4 times of the length of the first (center) vertical line on the projected lines' side. Use your scale ruler to center this second vertical line on the horizon line, and make sure that its top point and bottom points touch the top line and the bottom line of the projected perspective lines. In our example's case, this means a 22.4' vertical line in 1/4" scale. We even it up to 23' for easier processing.

Tip: Evening up your number is encouraged with this method.

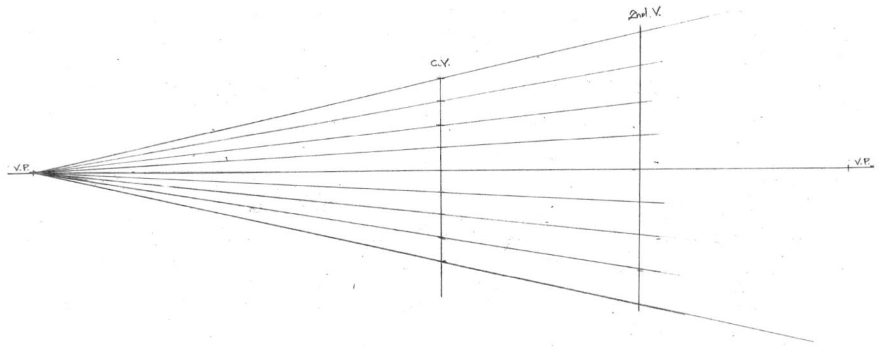

Tip: The tricky part of this method is to remember that you always use the vanishing point at the other side of the center vertical line to set up your side grid's perspective lines.

- Step 3:

  Draw a diagonal line, from corner to corner, between the first vertical line and the second one. Then, draw vertical lines at every point where the diagonal line crosses the projected perspective lines. Now, you have one side of the perspective grid set up.

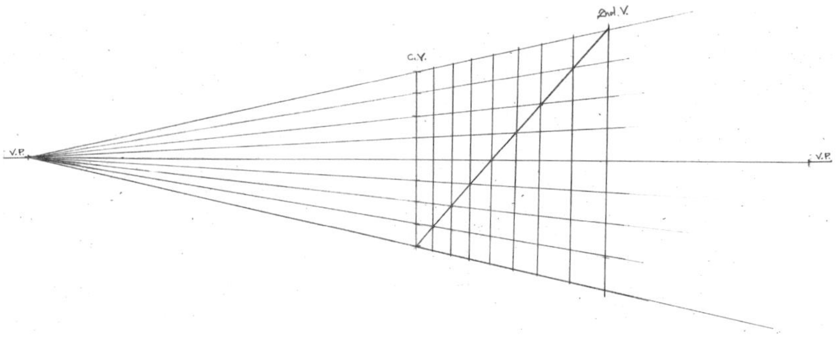

- Step 4:

  Repeat Steps 2 and 3 to set up the grid on the other side of the first vertical line.

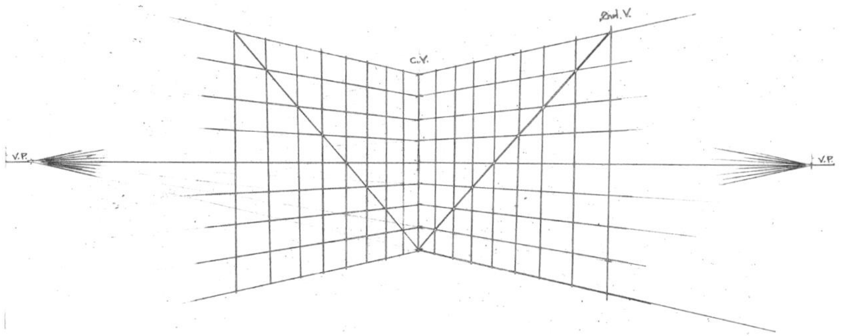

- Step 5:

  Project out from the two vanishing points through the bottom row of crossing points on both side grids to make a grid on the floor. (You can draw a top grid in the same way as well, if you need to draw perspective details at the ceiling area.)

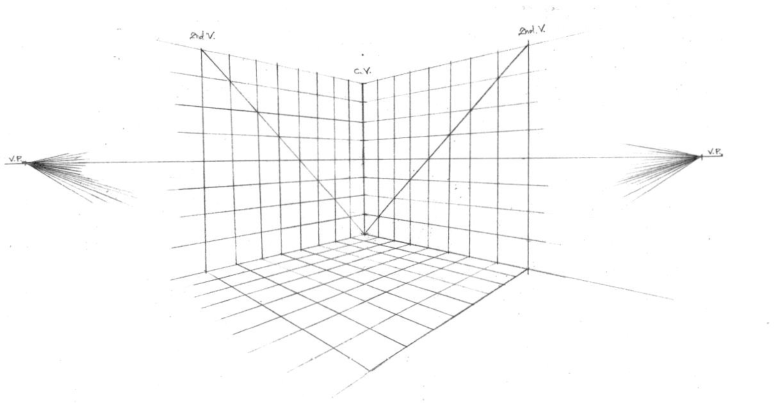

Modifying/Adjusting the Grid to Match Your Needs

This is a similar process to what we discussed earlier with modifying the grid for one vanishing point perspective.

Add Extensions to the Grid

Draw a diagonal line from corner to corner of an existing square on the perspective grid at the edge of the side grid which you want to extend, and project it out. Then, project all of the nearby side grid's perspective lines out. Add vertical lines at those newly formed crossing points where the new diagonal line meets those newly extended perspective lines.

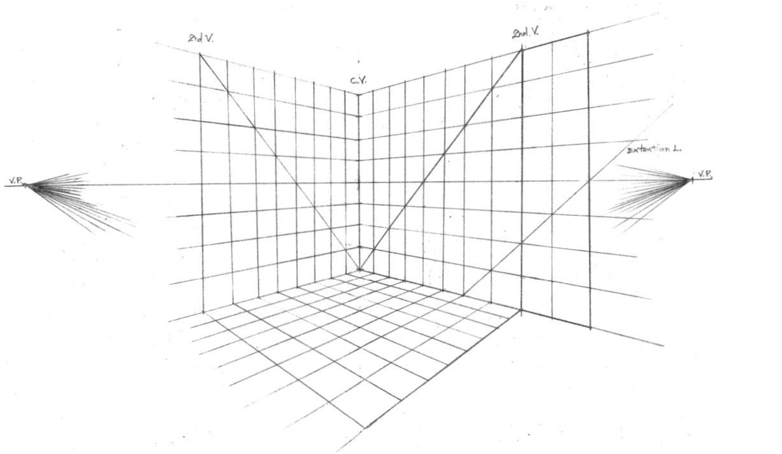

Draw a Two Vanishing Points Perspective Drawing with a Floor Plan

- Step 1:

  Draw a scaled floor plan of the set you are going to do. It needs to have a grid over it in the same grid layout as the perspective grid you are preparing. In our example: 2' for each square on the grid.

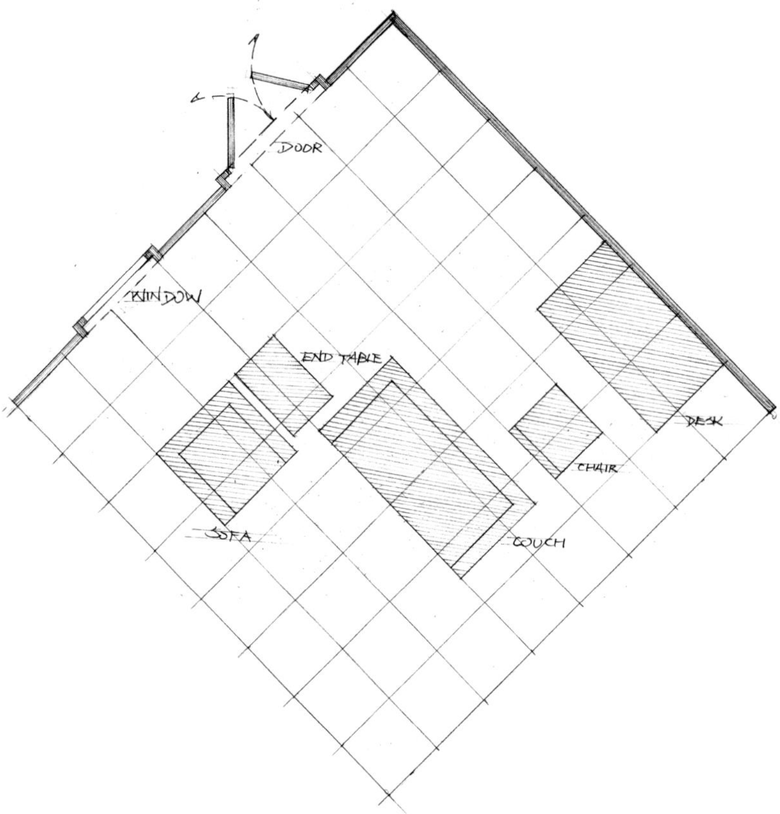

- Step 2:

  Count the squares on the gridded floor plan, then, put the walls and major architecture elements (like the doors, the window, etc.) into the perspective grid, according to their locations on the gridded floor plan. For example, count the squares on the gridded floor plan from the front line and from the side wall for the object's floor footprint positions, and how many squares from the floor to reach their positions in height at the side grids. Then, draw furniture pieces in as "cubes" to fit them into the perspective grid with their positions, sizes, and basic perspective angles.

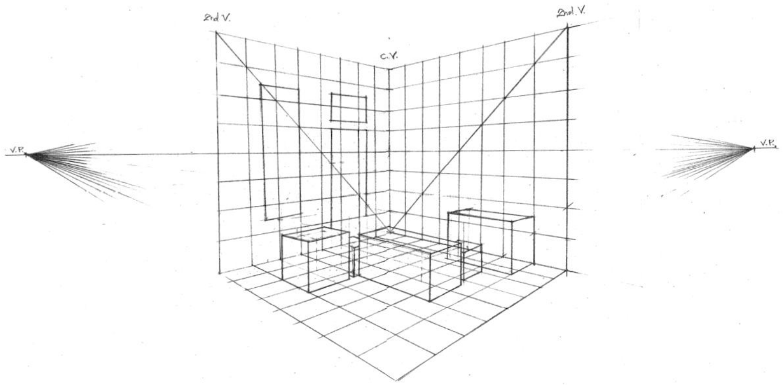

- Step 3:

  Carve details out of the "cubes." Erase the grid, and clean up the drawing for clarity. Enhance the drawing with drawing techniques: value contrast, shading, and texture.

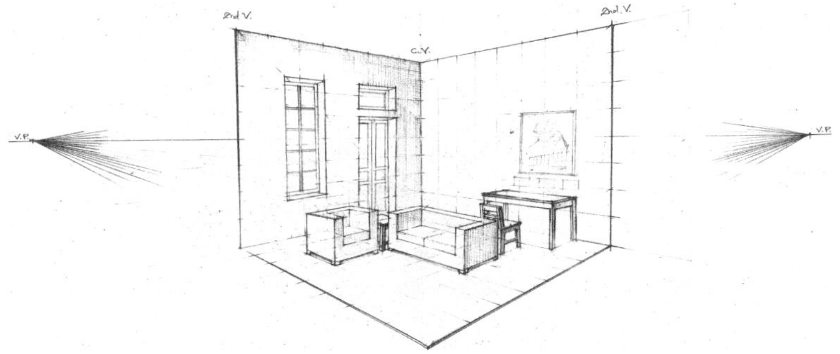

Tip: Always keep in mind the size you give to each square on the grid (the size each square represents), as you are drawing. In our example, each square stands for 2' in the physical world. So, a 1.5 grid represents 3'.

Working with a Pre-Made Two Vanishing Points Grid in Non-Proscenium Spaces

Not all theatres have prosceniums. The following two examples show step by step instructions on working with a pre-made two vanishing points grid in non-proscenium spaces.

UNWANTED TENDERNESS, New Jewish Theatre, 2005

Floor Plan

With this example, a pre-made two vanishing points grid PDF file was downloaded from the publisher's website (www.routledge.com/9780367860790). It is used to demonstrate how to modify a pre-made grid into a matching grid of the given space as needed and how to draw a set on a piece of vellum over it.

- Step 1:

Draw a floor plan for the show which you are working on. Then, draw a 2' grid on top of it (this can be done with a CAD program as well).

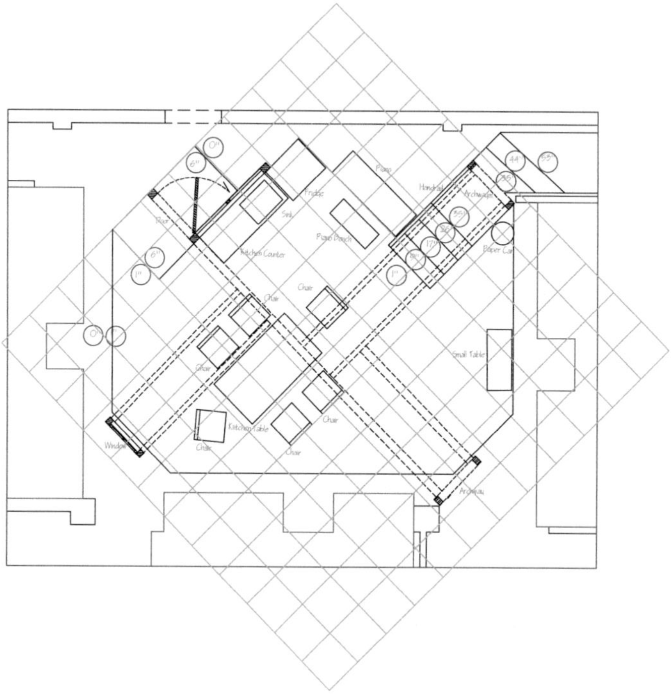

- Step 2:

Download a pre-made two points perspective grid PDF file from the publisher's web site (www.routledge.com/9780367860790), and print it out. Tape the printout and a sheet of vellum together at the top with the vellum on top.

On the vellum, modify the pre-made grid to the size you need for your set as discussed earlier (see "Add Extensions to the Grid").

Rough in your set pieces into the perspective grid by counting their positions on the gridded floor plan. Then, count the gridded floor plan for furniture cubes' positions and put them into the perspective grid.

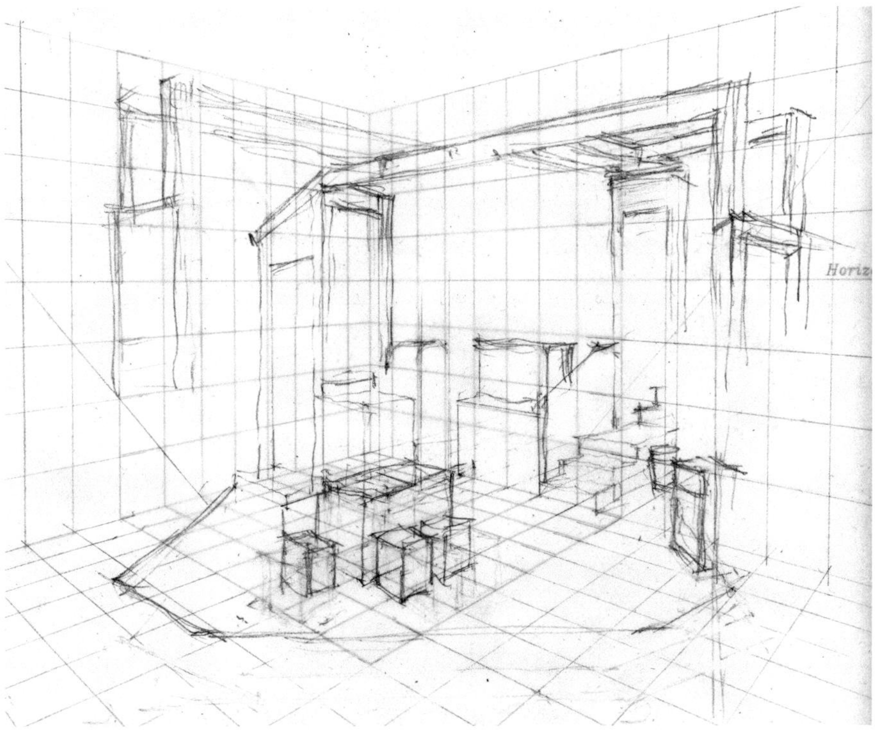

- Step 3:

  Put in details, clean up, and add in shading etc. to finish the set sketch.

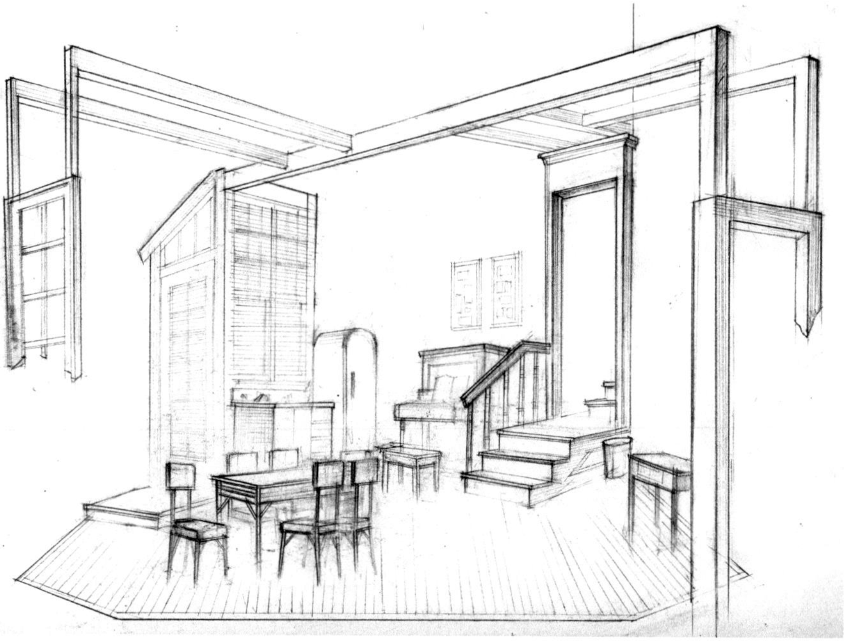

Tip:

When using pre-made grids over your floor plan, please ensure that you do the following.

The positions of your major set pieces on your perspective grid line up with their positions on the gridded floor plan.

Always tape the pre-made perspective grid printout and the vellum together with masking tape at the top. By taping them together, you avoid position mismatching as you keep working on and off with the project, while carrying your perspective drawing around.

CHAPTER 6

DRAWING TECHNIQUE

A handsome perspective drawing not only needs to make good on perspective and proportion, it also needs to be further enhanced with good drawing techniques. The most important techniques involved in making a good perspective drawing are: value enhancement, shading for clarity, and adding visual texture.

HATCHING AND VISUAL TEXTURE

Pencil movement on paper not only defines objects' shapes, it can also work in dimensional quality and sketched texture to illustrate an object's features and, more importantly, to give your drawing good presentational quality. Solid black shadows are not recommended in perspective drawings. When drawing shadows, hatching is recommended. The type of hatching is always associated with the object's key features which you are trying to communicate. Drawing visual texture in your drawing is a fun and effective way to add more information and visual interest. Visual texture in drawing works on the principle of contrast. Visual texture can be applied during the shading process. It can be applied at both highlight areas and shadow areas, as long as enough contrast could be established with the neighboring areas.

Below are some typical pencil hatching patterns (all done with a #2 pencil):

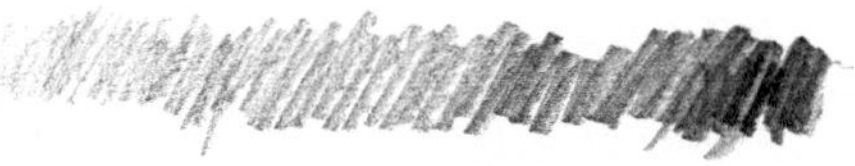	Your pencil strokes' values could be changed by varying the pressure you put on the pencil.
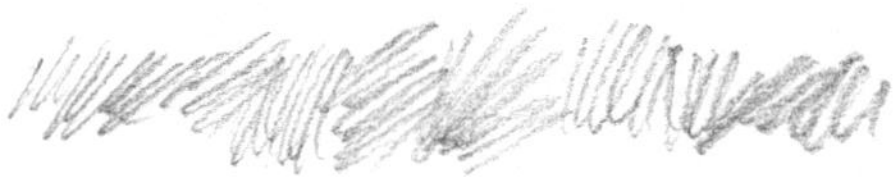	Changing the direction of your pencil strokes could add visual interest.

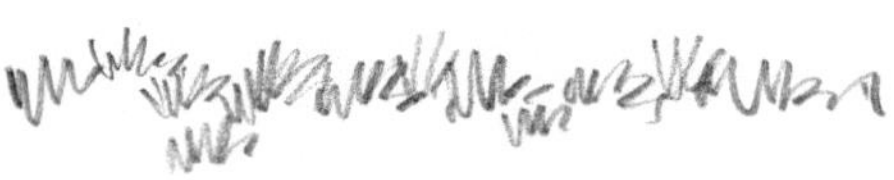	Organizing your pencil strokes to give them different texture features (in this case, visualizing grass).
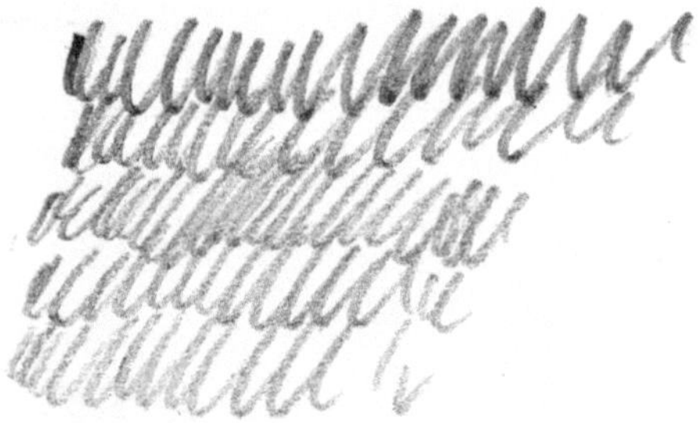	Repetition can make a pattern as texturing.
	Dark to light consistent strokes simulates natural value fading.
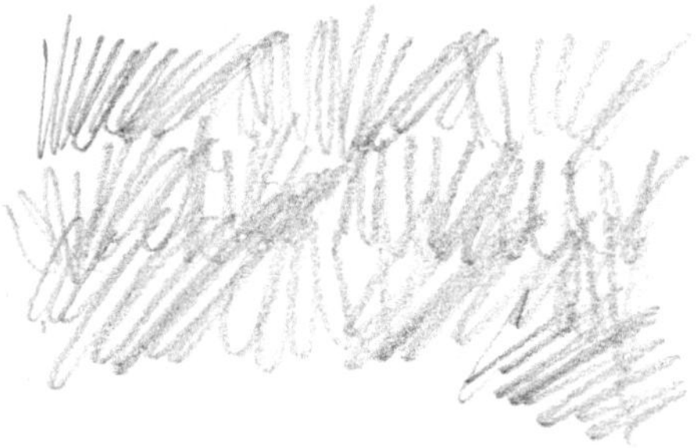	Loosely organized pencil strokes give a lightly "airy" feel.
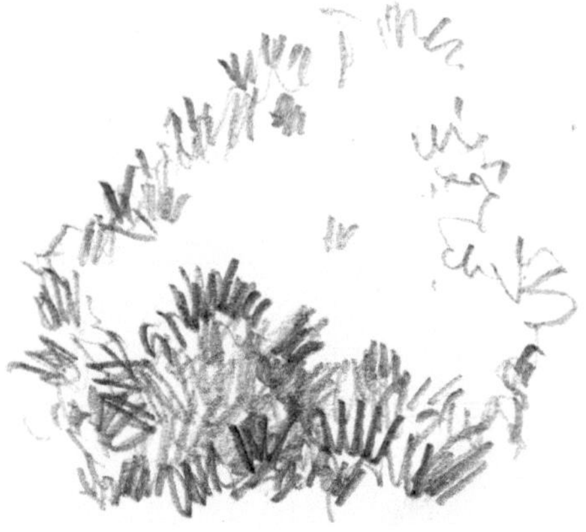	Organize pencil strokes direction to create shadows and highlights.

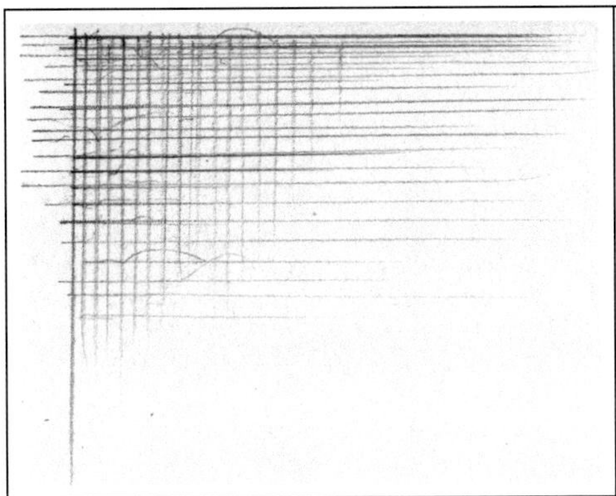	Drawing pencil strokes with a ruler is an effective technique borrowed from hand drafting. It works especially well with drawing platforms, steps, and other similar objects.
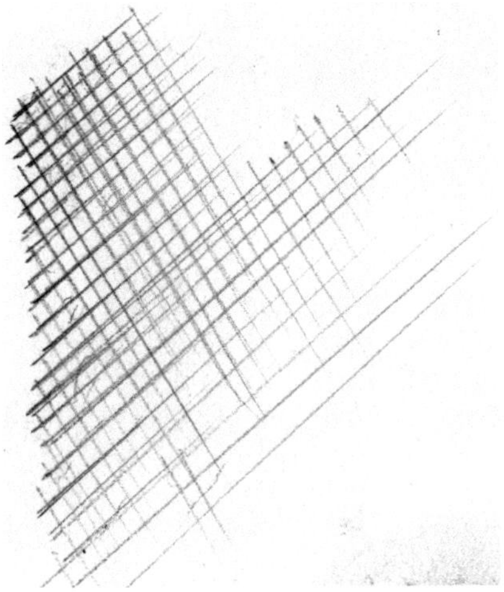	Pencil stroke hatching with a ruler at an angle adds visual interest.
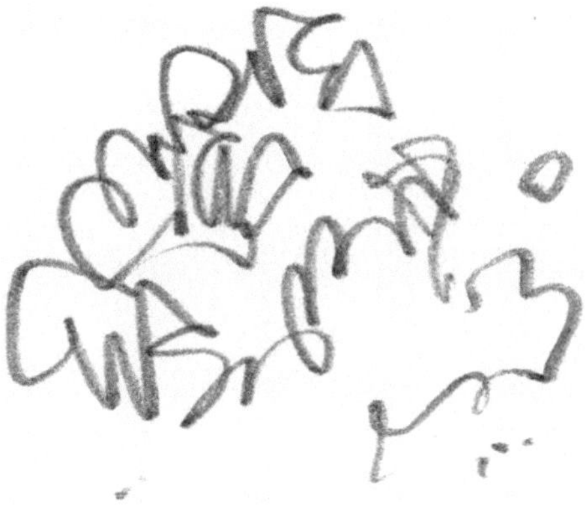	Freehand pencil strokes work for special textures, such as foliage.

On the next page is an example of how drawing techniques help to improve the look of a perspective sketch, showing the techniques discussed above, including using freehand pencil lines to make a foliage texture.

TALLEY'S FOLLY, New Jewish Theatre, 2004

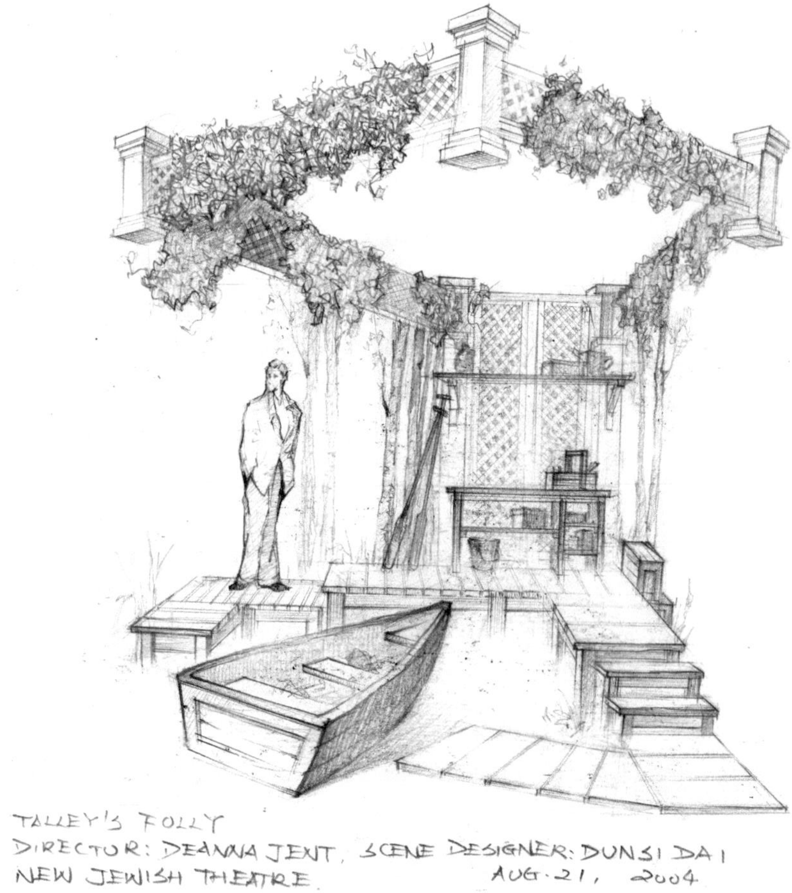

Tip: Organize pencil strokes as visual texture. Try to turn your pencil strokes about 90 degrees to the object's natural direction. It usually looks better.

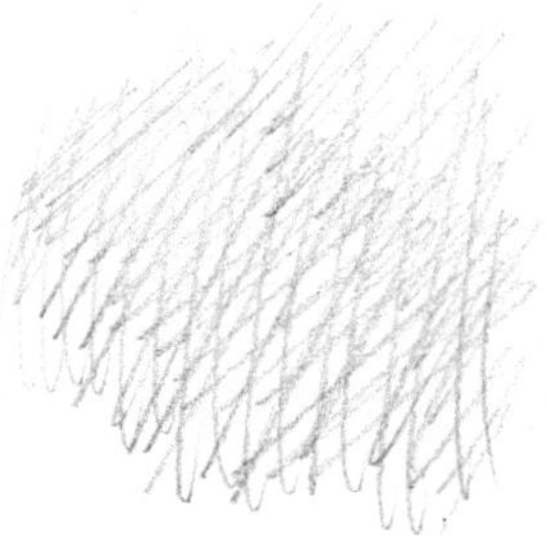

Using erasers as a drawing tool can create special effects, such as with mirror, light effect, diffused haze, etc.

When working with an eraser, start with a medium value background.

	Do some pencil hatching in the targeted area first. Then, smudge it with your fingers. Cut your eraser with an executive knife (or matte knife) to get a sharp edge, then, make negative strokes on the smudged area. Retractable eraser pens can do this job as well.
	If a large area needs to be lightened up, hatch the area with your eraser.

VALUE ENHANCEMENT

In drawing terms, values deal with blackness and whiteness and are established through contrast. Working on value contrast is an effective way to enhance a perspective drawing. When we look at an object, it appears sharper, clearer, and in higher contrast when it gets closer to us; and it appears blurrier and in lower contrast when it moves away from us. In perspective drawings, we can manipulate this perception to further enhance our drawing's perspective illusion:

Use sharper and darker lines for objects in the foreground, and fade them into blurry and lighter lines with less contrast in the background. It brings a much needed "airy" feel into perspective drawings.

In creating this contrast, we need to pay attention to how we establish value in step terms. It is very important to realize that there are many "steps" from black to white in value within a given sketch, mostly shown as different shades of gray. If you could work out at least five such steps into your drawing in value contrast, your drawing will look good. If you could work seven or more such steps into your drawing, your drawing will look very sophisticated. Value steps work like musical notes to charm your viewers.

In my drawing practice, I always make the downstage corners of the set pieces darker and more sharply defined (by pressing down on the #2 pencil harder), and let those extended lines fade away into the distance by reducing the pressure on the pencil. This helps to "pull" the corners out and send the other parts away in perspective illusion.

> *Tip: For clarity, it is very important to have a focus in your drawing. Your drawing needs to be in sharp contrast with clarity in your focused area. For the rest, you can loosen them up and bring some "air" into your drawing, and make it appear less rigid. This will not only save you drawing time, but it also will make your drawing appear to have more "life" in it.*

The scene design perspective sketch below demonstrates how the pencil techniques discussed above are used in a real set design sketch.

ON STRIVERS ROW, Stony Brook Theatre, 1994

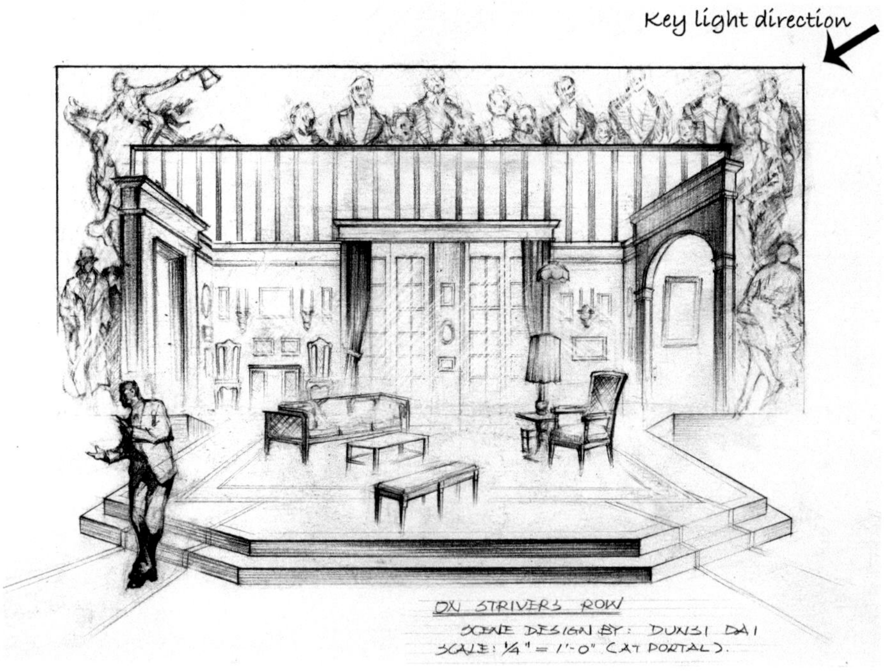

SHADING FOR CLARITY

Shading is a process of working out shadows and highlights. Establishing shadow and highlight helps your perspective drawing look more dimensional and appear to be more "finished." Shading also helps to clarify relationships among objects to improve the perspective illusion.

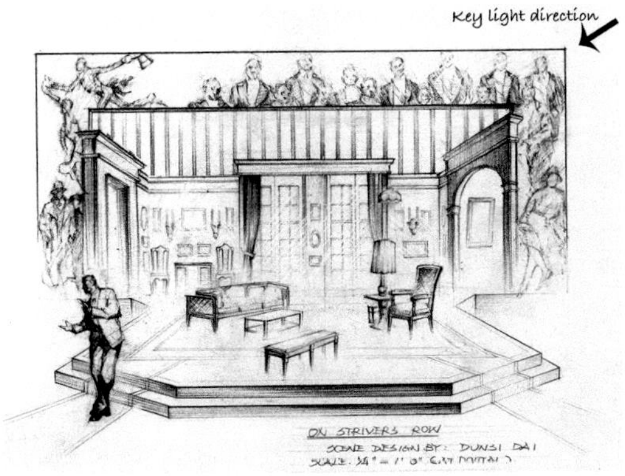

When you are working on shading, the first thing to do is to establish a "key light" direction in your drawing. Key light is the dominant light in a given moment. Use the key light direction as the guide to organize highlight and shadow areas for consistency.

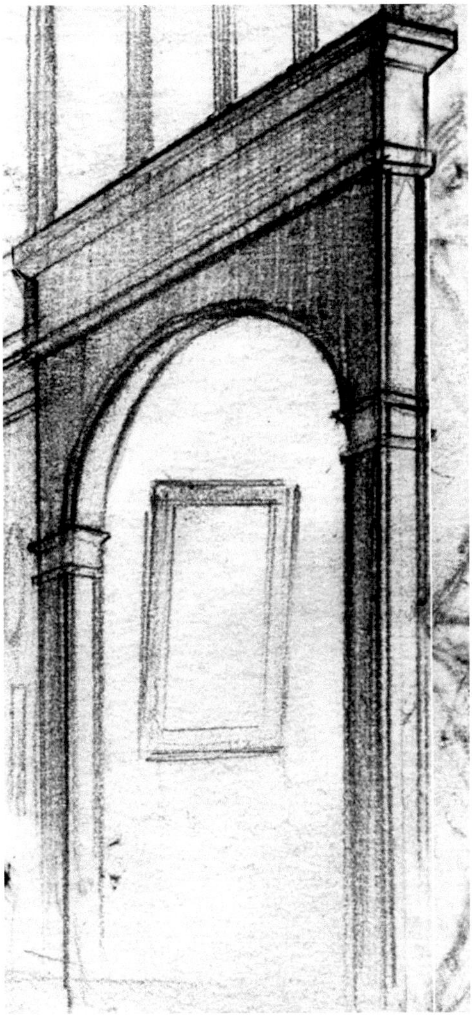

When doing shading, the most common trap that a beginning designer may fall into is making the shadows too dark, appearing in solid black. This mostly results from trying to match the value contrast you see in a photo research. It is important to realize that you are working on a perspective sketch, not on copying a photo. Clear information and a handsome presentation are much more important than photorealistically copying your photo research. In a drawing, hatched lines allow you to build up your value, layer by layer in establishing value steps. You will also need to consider the effect of reflective light (light bouncing from the stage floor, etc.) on stage, as well as other preferred stage light effects. Working on those considerations helps to reduce those "dead" (solid black) shadow areas and brings more "life" into your drawing.

USING AN ERASER AS A DRAWING TOOL

The action of subtracting (especially partial subtracting) is a very valuable way to adjust your drawing. It can give your drawing some desired special effects. Thus, an eraser can serve as an effective negative drawing tool.

- Adjusting value.

  Use an eraser to lighten up your drawing, especially the shaded areas.

- Adding visual texture.

  You will be pleasantly surprised to find out how many visual texture effects can be created by using an eraser. Below are some typical examples.

- Always using cross-strokes (negative hatching).

  An eraser works best as a negative drawing tool when you use it with cross-strokes. As you work on crossing strokes with your eraser, you will find out that an eraser with a sharp edge is much more desirable. This can be achieved by cutting your eraser with a sharp knife (like an executive knife). It gives you the ability to subtract the value from your drawing gradually with thin negative hatched lines. You will also be able to control how much you want to lighten an area up and how fuzzy you want a part of the image to look.

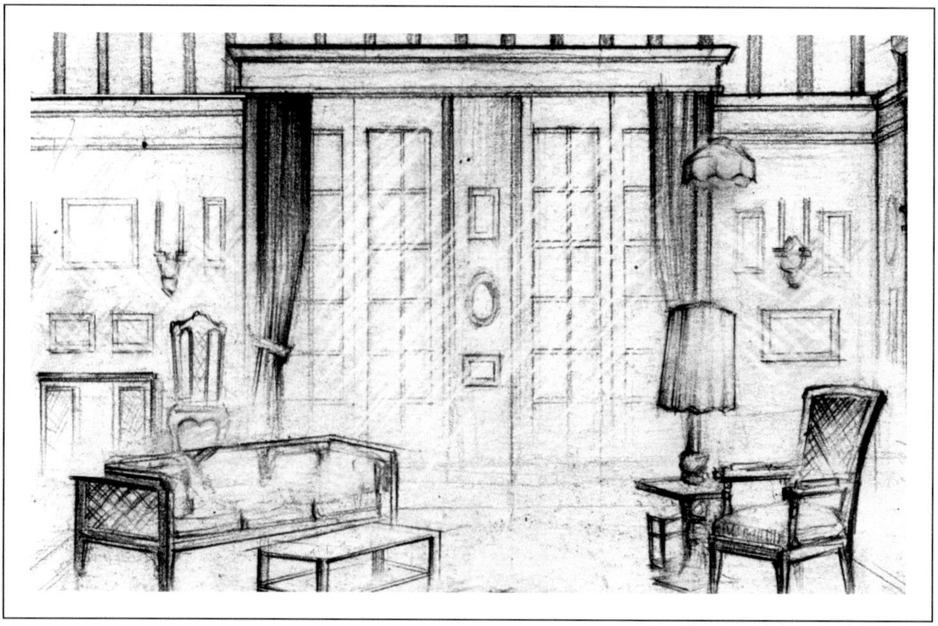

FINISH THE PERSPECTIVE DRAWING

Finishing a perspective drawing is a process of enhancing its presentational quality and cleaning up the smudges and unwanted lines, then seal the drawing with a layer of Clear Matte Finish.

- Step 1:

  Further adjust contrast from the overall view. In most cases, darken and sharpen lines on selected objects to clarify their shapes and perspective relationships.
- Step 2:

  Clean up unwanted smudges and anything you do not think belongs to this drawing with an eraser.
- Step 3:

  Label your drawing with show-related information: play's title, playwright's name, director's name, scene designer's name, theatre's name, date, etc. (pay attention to give credit for formal presentations).
- Step 4:

  Spray a layer of finish, such as Krylon (or 3M) Clear finish to seal the drawing. Matte finish is recommended. Do not over spray and make sure to spray in an open and well-ventilated area. Caution: Only seal your drawing after you are certain you are done with the sketch (i.e. no more changes are expected, and the design has been approved). This step will make any further changes to the drawing much more difficult. A common practice is to wait until the show opens, then seal the sketch.

CHAPTER 7

PERSPECTIVE DRAWING METHOD II: FRAME METHOD

The Frame Method, by its nature, is a loosely established reference system. You set up a reference "frame," which gives you a set of relatively "measureable" reference marks to base your perspective drawing from. For the scenery pieces near this frame, you can refer to the marks at the frame directly to get some measurable information. For the scenery pieces away from the frame, you will estimate them by using the perspective principles with your experience in perspective drawing: all perspective lines end at vanishing point(s) on the horizon line; those objects coming toward you will grow in size, while those pieces moving away from you will shrink in size, etc. Always draw an actor figure in simple lines right next to the frame to be used as a proportional reference. This actor figure appears much more natural and direct when you are looking for a reference for estimating proportional relationship on stage.

To use this method, the user needs to have some basic training in drawing, with a good understanding of the cube system introduced in Chapter 4. It could be a little more challenging to master (compared with using the Grid Method). The advantage is that it gives you much more freedom and helps you to draw much faster. It can work with any perspective type, including one vanishing point perspective, two vanishing points perspective, and multi-vanishing points perspective, without changing the basic frame set-up.

Choose a scale (1/2", 1/4", or 3/16"), which will help you to fit your drawing within the paper size of your choice. With your scale ruler, use the given theatre's measurement information to establish a reference frame in height and width. This frame is usually the given theatre's proscenium opening's measurements. If the theatre space you are working in is a proscenium stage with a thrust, you still can set up this frame at the proscenium. If you are working in a flexible studio theatre (a black box theatre), you can set up this "frame" position anywhere. (It could be set up downstage at the edge of the acting area or at the back wall/backdrop position.) Ideally, you should set this reference frame closer to the most important set piece in order to make your reference marks more directly comparable to the most important scenery pieces. No real theatre architectural details are needed for creating this frame. Keep in mind that this reference frame should always relate to a fixed position on your floor plan.

The following is a sketch which we use to illustrate the procedure of using such a frame at a proscenium stage.

QUEEN OF SHEBA, St. Louis Black Rep, 1998
Floor Plan:
Make sure your floor plan is in scale. Putting a grid over it (optional) can help you see the proportional relationship more clearly among the set pieces.

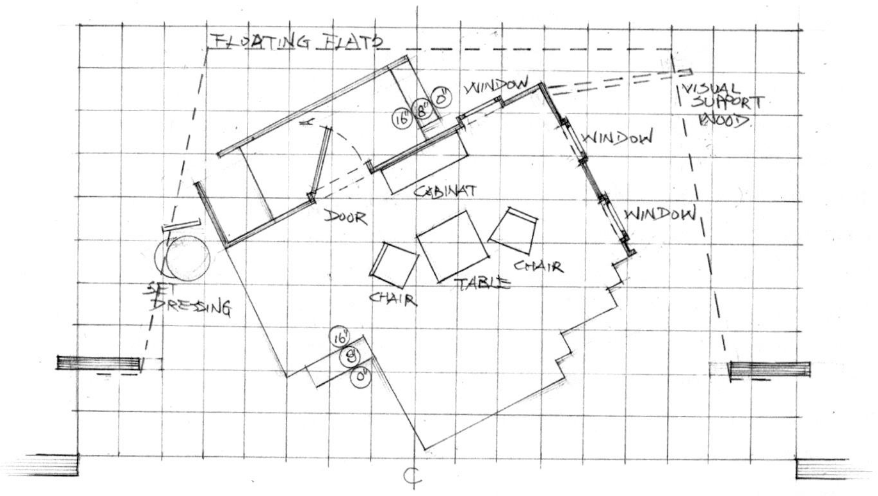

FRAMING METHOD DRAWING PROCEDURE

- Step 1:
  - Our example uses a space with a proscenium opening of 36' x 20'. The grid on the floor plan is at 2' for each square. Draw a 36' x 20' rectangle in a scale of your choice (our example uses ¼" scale). This is your drawing's reference frame. Mark

this "frame," with your scale ruler, at every 2' on one side and at the bottom. Also, mark its center-line position. Those marks will serve as our reference points, and you will use them for proportional estimation references.

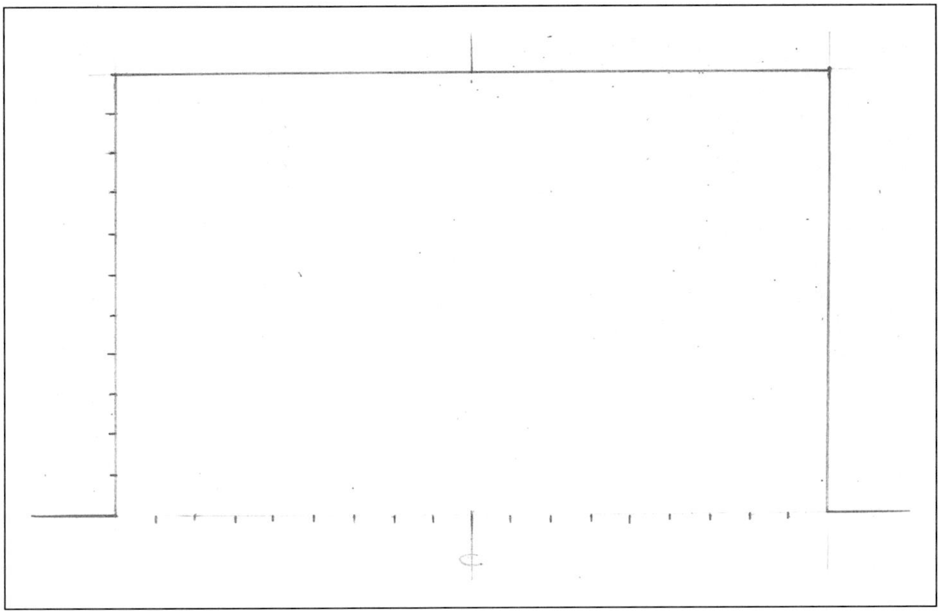

Tip: You really can set your marks in any size (such as making each mark at every 1' or 4'). In general, too many reference marks tend to be more confusing than helpful. For most of my professional design sketches, I usually use 3' as the reference marks' size for large show, and use 2' reference marks for small shows.

- Step 2:

  Set your horizon line (i.e. the viewer's eye level) at 3' high above the theatre deck if you do not have too much to show on your stage floor (in many theatres, this assumes the viewer is sitting in the fifth row). You could set your horizon line higher, if you have much to communicate about your stage floor design and levels. In this case, your horizon line could be set at 6' (or even higher as needed). This assumes the viewer is sitting in the tenth row in many theatre auditoriums, where most of the directors/stage managers set up their work tables during the tech/dress rehearsal. Setting your horizon line between 3' and 6' helps to make your drawing appear in a standard perspective view.

Tip: Avoid putting your "viewer" in the balcony (do not set your horizon line above the top of your set's major walls, nor higher than the top of the proscenium opening). It may look odd and unnatural.

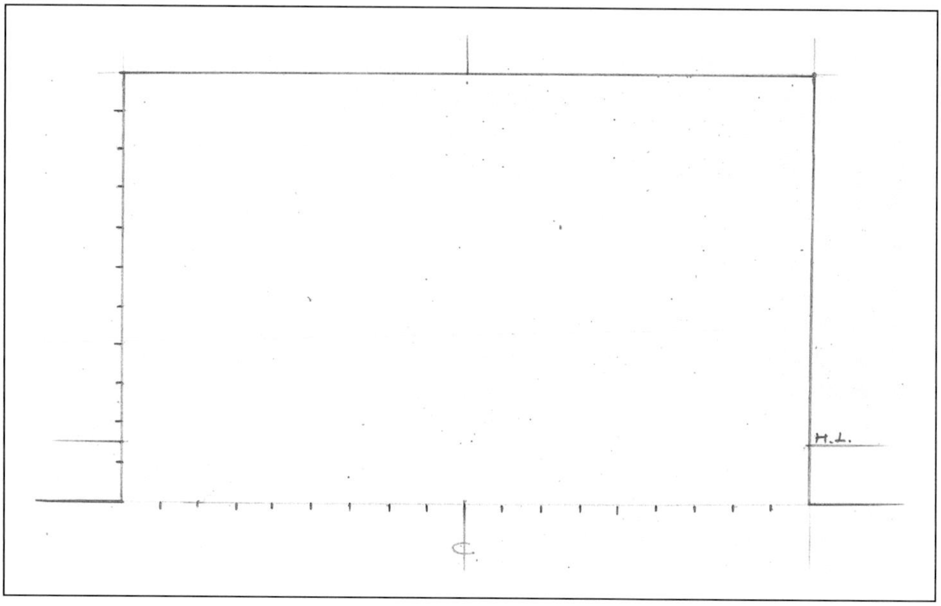

- Step 3:

  Draw an actor figure in simple lines right next to your marked frame, and use your scale ruler to make sure he/she is at 6' tall.

  This helps you to visualize the utmost reference on the stage: the actor's size. This figure will serve as a more direct proportional reference as you move forward. Everything you draw will be compared to this simple line figure for a quick proportional check. This is based on the common understanding that everything we make on the stage will be put to a proportional test against the actor automatically.

- Step 4:

  Rough in your set pieces proportionally as they appear on the floor plan:

  - Look for the proportional relationship between the wall/object you are drawing and its neighbors. Use the reference marks on the frame to help with proportional estimates.

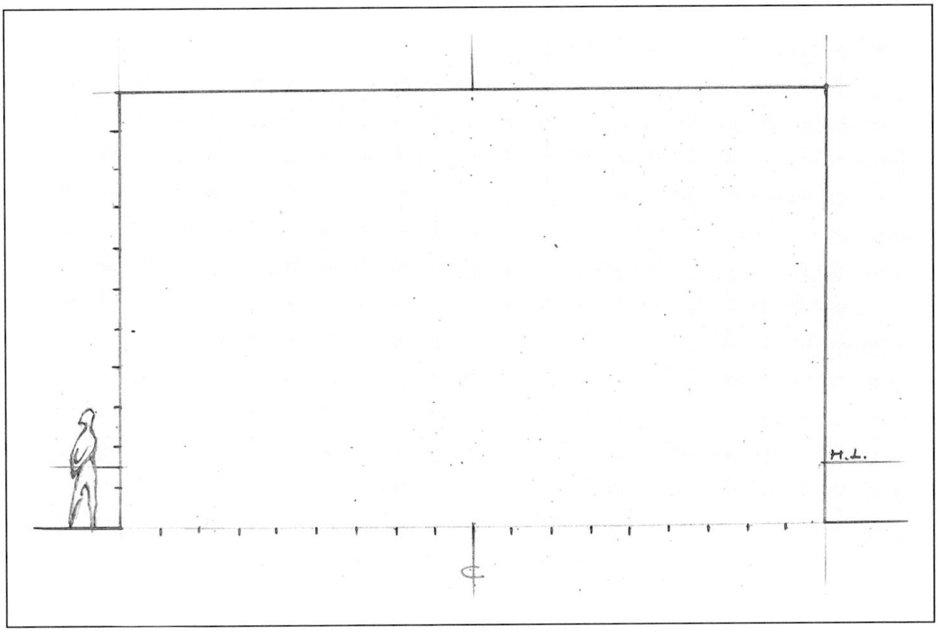

- Look for the proportional relationship between the wall/ object you are drawing to the 6' tall actor figure at the "frame" positon, and further adjust your proportional estimations.
- Use the 6' tall actor figure at the "frame" position as a base reference to further estimate and set up key architecture elements' sizes, such as door, archway, window, and major furniture pieces. Use cubes to establish furniture pieces.

Tip: Remind yourself that all vanishing points need to end at the horizon line, relatively speaking. Pay attention to the overall visual composition. When you are unsure about a given set piece's size, always check with the marks on the "frame" and the actor figure at the frame for reference.

Tip: You will need to estimate a lot. As you know that you can trust your measureable reference frame directly only in the area right next to it. So, refer to your frame to set up those set pieces near the frame first, in height and width. For set pieces away from the frame, remember that they will grow in size as they come toward you and will shrink in size as they move away. This estimating procedure is a fun game, and it will require some practice in order to feel comfortable with it. Again, always keep their proportional relationships as shown in the floor plan.

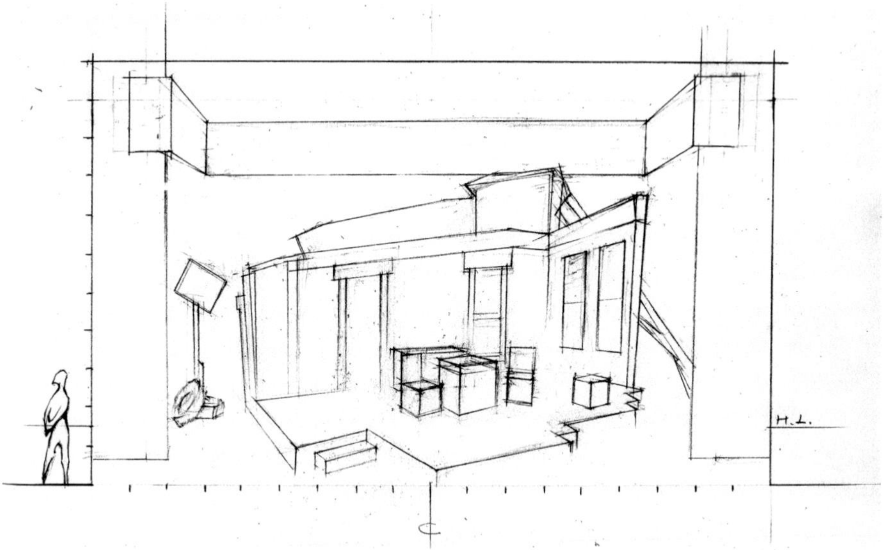

The picture below illustrates how your actor reference figure works as you process forward with your perspective drawing with the frame method.

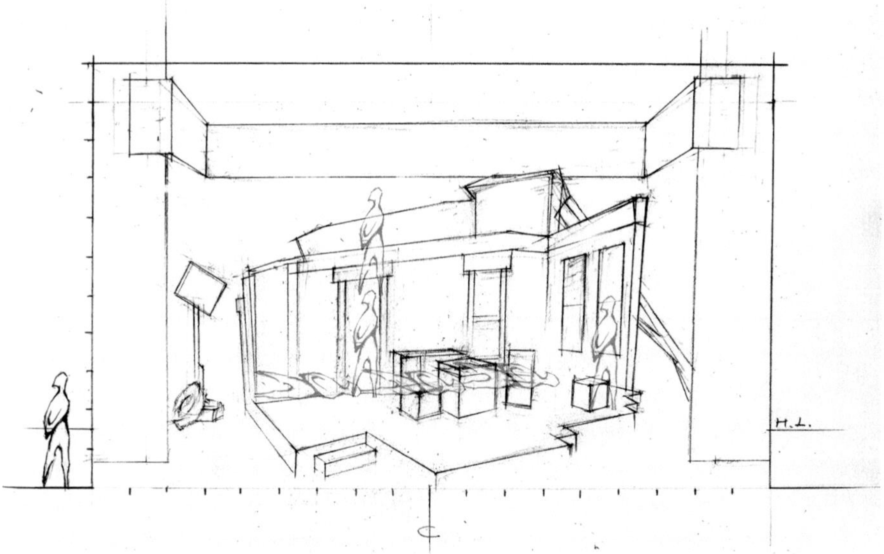

Please pay attention: the actor figures at the back wall have been shrunk in size with estimated perspective consideration.

- Step 5:

  Carve out details from the cubes to bring their true looks out. Keep adjusting size, shape, and details, as you move forward, and keep referring to those marks on the reference frame and to the reference actor with proportional size estimation. Erase both the reference marks and the cube lines to clean up the drawing. Enhance the drawing with drawing techniques: value contrast, shading, and visual texture, etc.

  This is a tricky stage. You need to refer to your visual research for your set piece's details. At the same time, keep reminding yourself to double-check with the reference frame for proportional adjustment.

Tip: A designer's perspective sketch is like an art project. Trust your trained perspective common sense. Feeling right is more important than having all perspective lines end at exactly the desired vanishing points. We are drawing with a lot of estimations. This understanding will help you be more adventurous in your drawing process and less being bogged down by the worries of pursuing a "perfect" perspective.

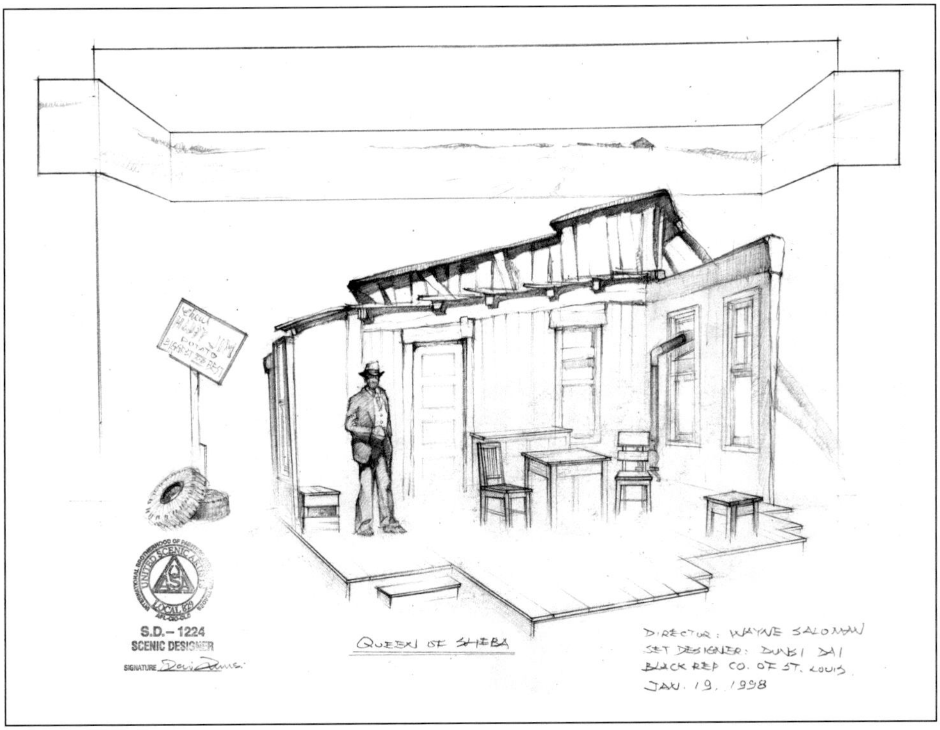

WORKING WITH FRAME METHOD IN NON-PROSCENIUM SPACES (SMALL SET)

TALLY'S FOLLY, New Jewish Theatre, 2004
Floor Plan:

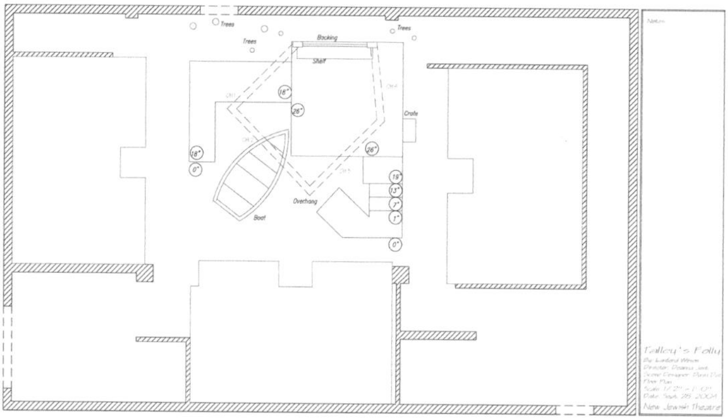

- Step 1:

  Set up a reference frame based on the floor plan. You can choose to set up this frame at any point. In practical terms, it works better to set it up near the objects which most easily relates it to those important pieces on the set. In this example, I choose to set up the reference frame next to the steps. Mark this frame at every 2'. For this small theatre space, I choose to have a 16' x 14' frame. Then, draw a 6' tall actor figure next to the frame for further reference.

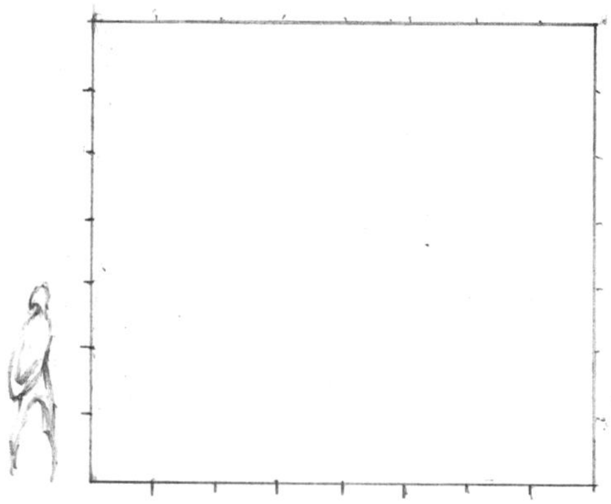

- Step 2:

  Rough in the set, using both the marks on the frame and the actor figure as proportional references. The multiple figures in the drawing below demonstrate how this process works out (with proportional reference).

Tip: Notice how the actor figures' sizes at the back wall position have been shrunk, and the one at down stage has been enlarged, comparing with the actor figure standing next to the reference frame. This is an example of applying perspective principle and common sense in estimating perspective proportionally.

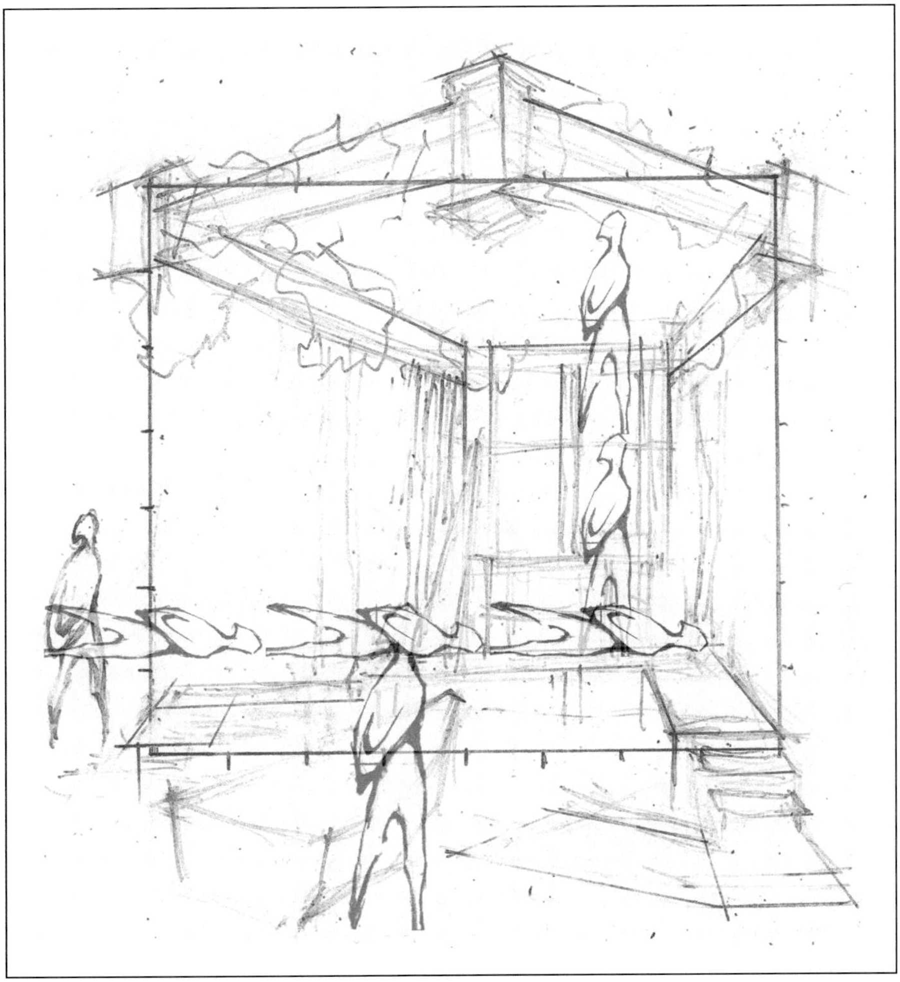

- Step 3:

  Put in details and work with drawing techniques to finish the sketch.

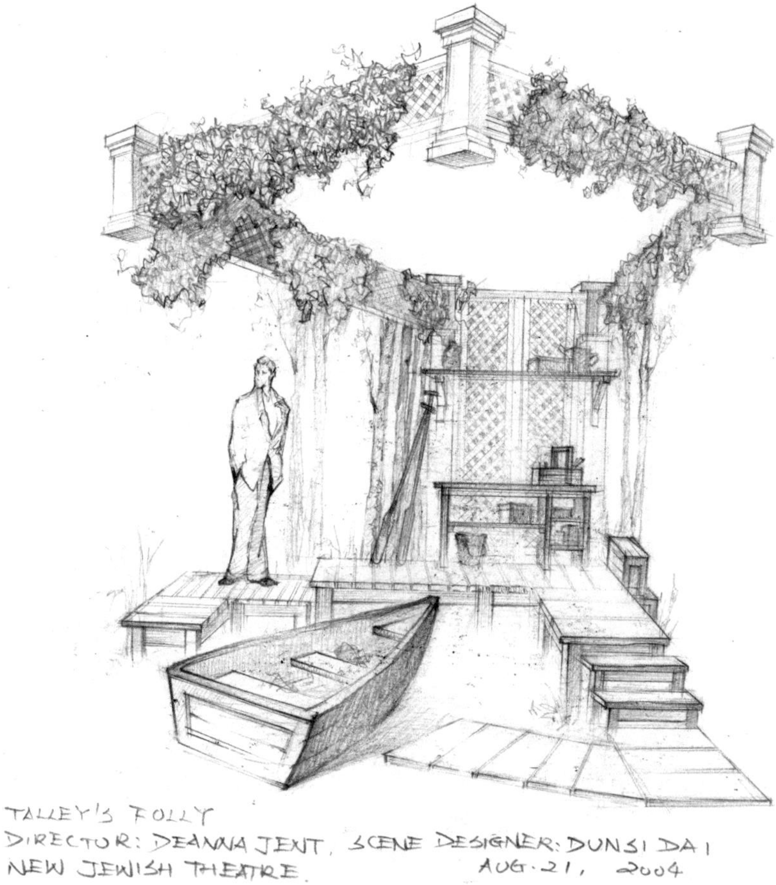

WORKING WITH FRAME METHOD IN NON-PROSCENIUM SPACES (LARGE SET)

RIVER NIGER, St. Louis Black Rep, 2004
Floor Plan:

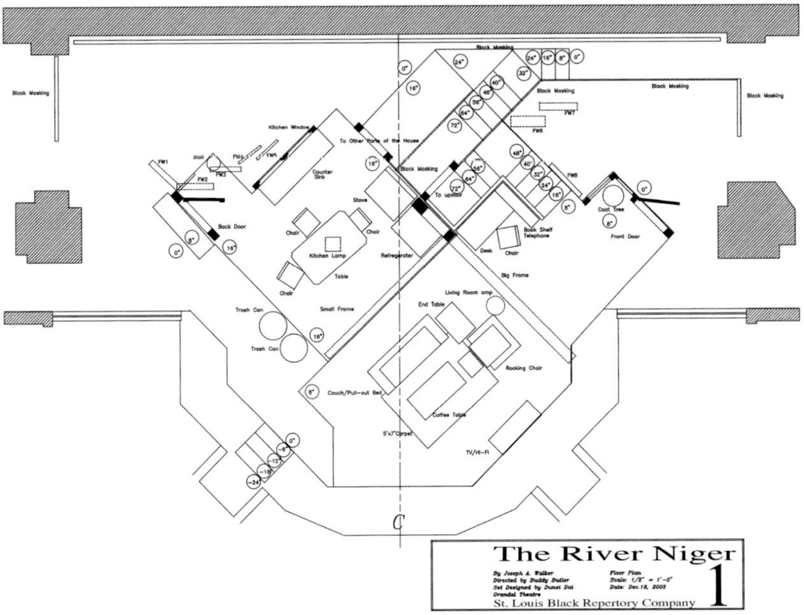

- Step 1:

  Set up a frame based on the floor plan. This theatre was converted from an old church. It has a sort of a proscenium feel without a physical proscenium (it has side pillar positions, without a top part). It has a large thrust. It looks better to set our reference frame at the pillar position, since it is at the middle point of the set and therefore is easier to estimate perspective and make proportional adjustments of set pieces in front and behind it. Plus, that frame position is close to the door at stage left and the door at stage right. We can use them as further reference by using our knowledge of standard door sizes. This space's stage opening is at 46' in width, with a grid at 21' in height. So, I choose to draw a frame of 46' x 22' to start.

  - Make marks every 2' (I chose to make marks at the frame top, since I know I will need to add in the thrust moving forward with this sketch).
  - Add in a 6' actor figure next to the frame, and mark the center line position (it will come in handy when doing proportional estimating later).

Tip: Use a scale ruler to choose a proper scale. Consider the following factors:

- *Fit the frame within your paper size.*
- *Fit the sketch in the paper with a nice composition (do not draw a sketch which is too small compared to the given paper size).*

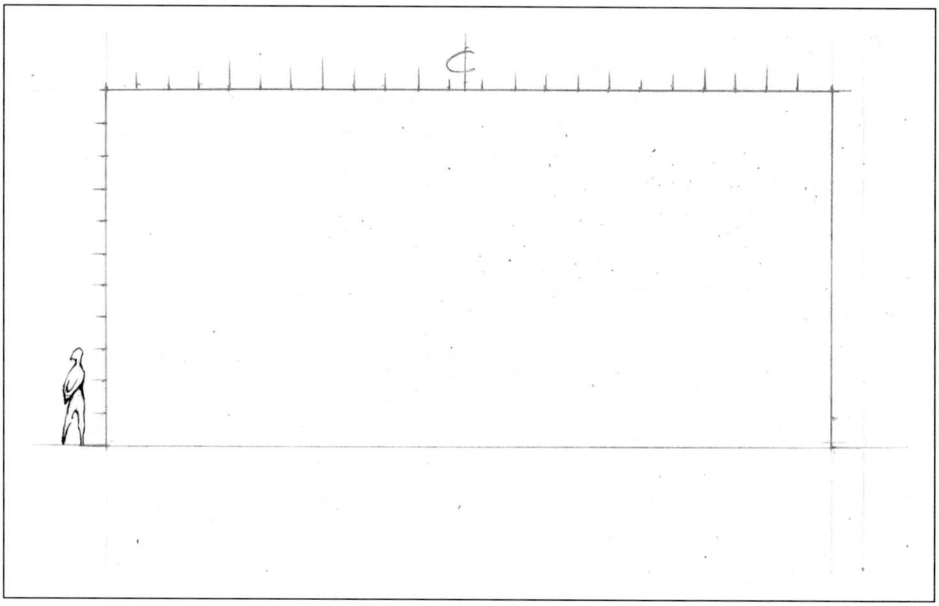

- Step 2:

  Rough in the set and the thrust stage:

  Pay special attention to the proportional relationship between the stage, the thrust, and the set.

  Decide where your preferred horizon line is going to be set. Keep it at a fixed position.

  Refer to the center line and the marked frame to set the thrust and the basic set pieces' size, shape, and position proportionally.

  When in doubt about an object's size, refer to the actor's figure next to the frame to get a proportional hint (apply perspective principles and common sense; estimate within reason).

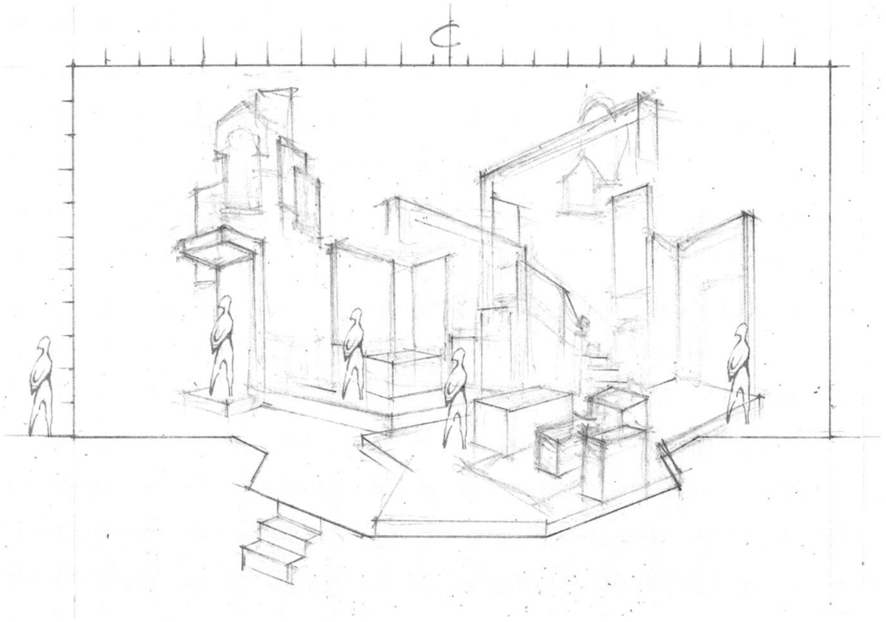

- Step 3:

  Put in details. Add shadows and highlights. Apply pencil techniques to enhance the perspective drawing's presentation quality (value contrast, hatching, etc.).

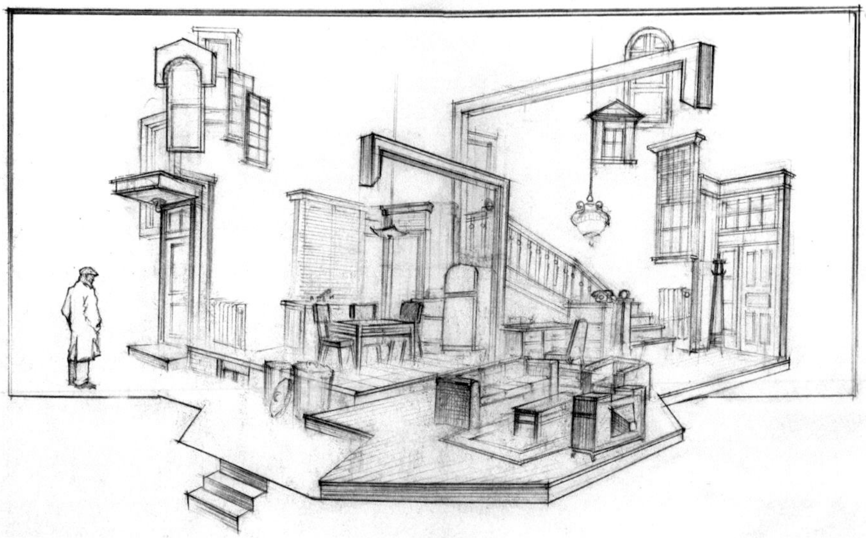

CHAPTER 8

PERSPECTIVE DRAWING METHOD III: FREEHAND WITH REFERENCES METHOD

After you have had some fun and feel really at home with the Frame Method, you may want to start doing more freehand work with only selective references while you work on perspective drawings. This is a true time saver, especially when you are designing in non-conventional spaces, such as an environmental theatre arrangement or an innovative space arrangement in a black box theatre. With this method, there is no need to draw grids nor a reference frame any more. Just keep your eye on a couple of selective references—in most cases, it is an actor figure in your drawing and the proportional relationships among the set pieces in your floor plan. In general, this method works best for small theatre spaces. (The Frame Method works well in both big and small theatre spaces.)

With this method, the major challenge is to keep your drawing in proportion relating to your floor plan. The key is to draw an actor in as soon as you put some basic set pieces into your drawing, and use this actor figure as your proportional reference to adjust the size of the set pieces around it. In doing so, you need to be very careful with the objects' proportional relationships. In most cases, your trained common sense in perspective (as you have developed in practicing the Grid Method and the Frame Method) will help you to work through the process successfully. This actor figure is the proportional anchor for your drawing.

The example below illustrates the procedure of the Freehand with References Method:

BIG RIVER, The Human Race Theatre, 2006

Floor Plan:

Pay special attention to the set pieces' and the furniture pieces' proportional relationships in the floor plan.

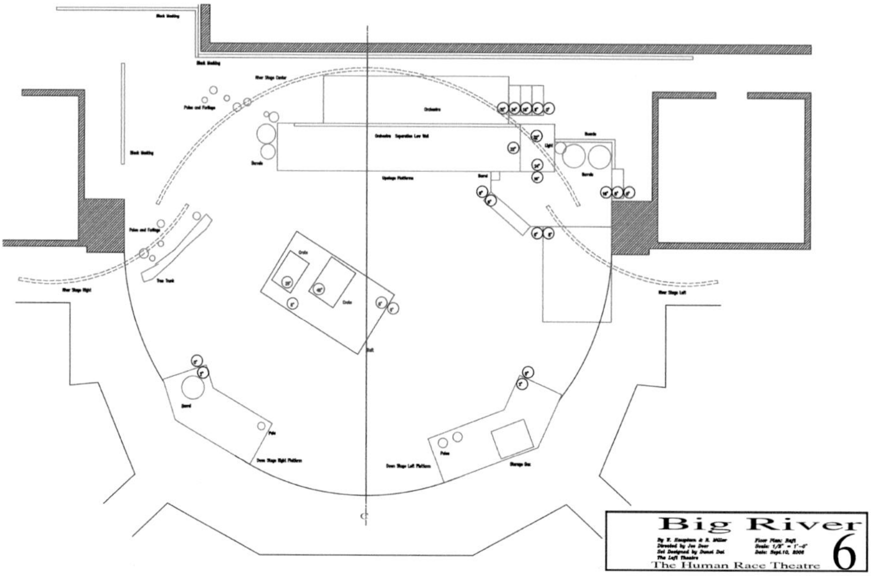

- Step 1:

  Draw an actor figure and freehand in your set pieces' basic shapes to form a visual composition. Pay special attention to the proportional relationships among the set pieces in the floor plan, as well as their proportional relationship to the actor figure.

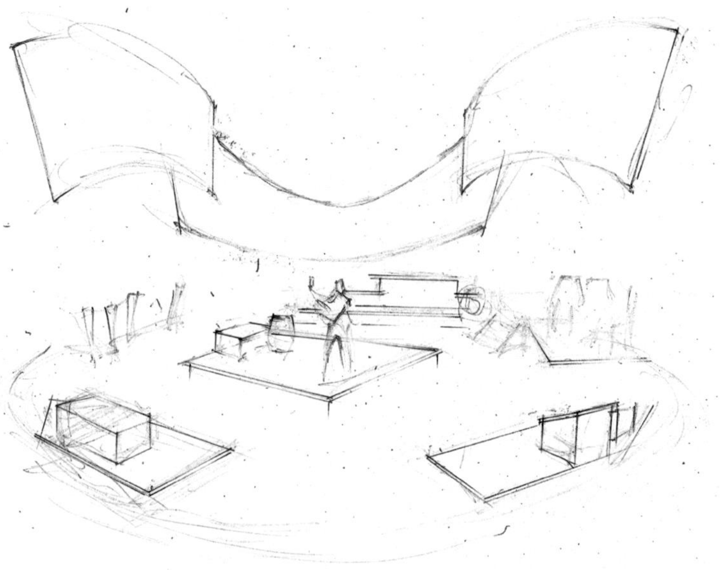

The picture below shows how the actor reference figure works as you progress with your perspective drawing in this method.

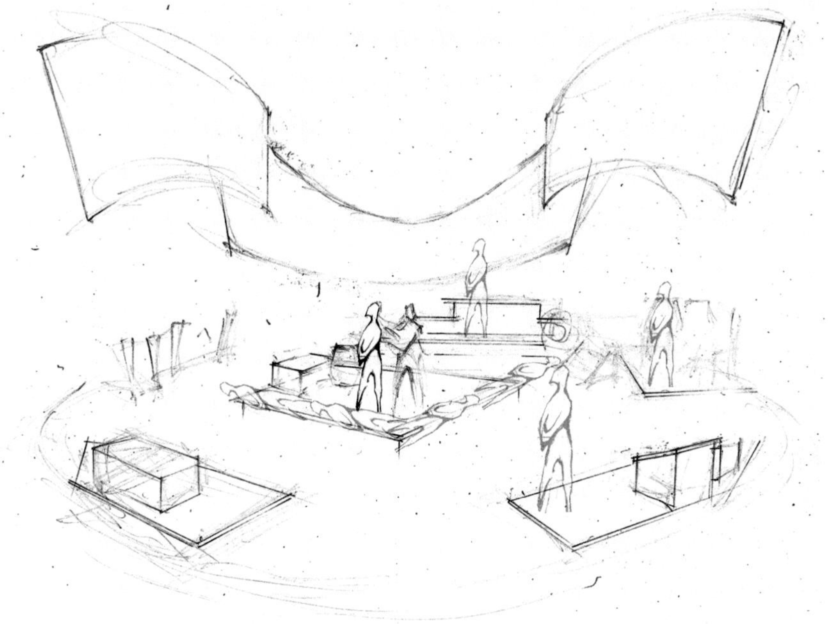

Please pay attention: *All actor reference figures have been adjusted in size with estimated perspective consideration.*

Tip: This is a tricky step because you need to estimate just about everything. You will mostly be guided by your trained perspective drawing experience. Your focus is on the overall visual composition and proportions (relating to the floor plan). You'll need more practice to feel comfortable with this method. Your previous experience with the Grid Method and the Frame Method will help you greatly with training your eye in viewing/predicting perspective adjustments. If you feel overwhelmed with this method, go back to the Frame Method for more practice. (You could stay with the Frame Method, if that makes you feel more at home.)

Tip: Use long lines, and generalize basic shapes in cube forms whenever needed. Try not to get into details at this step. This step focuses on estimating and adjusting the proportional relationship among the objects (based on the floor plan).

- Step 2:

  Use the proportional relationship established between the actor figure and his neighboring set pieces to further adjust the other set pieces and apply your trained perspective common sense (those perspective principles/elements) to your drawing. Use the cube system when encountering challenging objects. For example: Work out something from the set which could establish a basic proportional relation with the actor figure first. This is usually a door, an archway, or a large furniture piece which is easily relatable proportionally to the actor figure. This helps you further develop your major set piece in proportion to the neighboring areas. In our example's case, it is the raft and the crates on the raft.

Tip: When doing this, you need to relate the actor's size to an object's size which you can estimate with confidence. For example: a standard door's opening height is usually 6'–8", a desk is usually 3' high, and a chair is usually 18" high. Positioning your actor figure next to one of these objects will help set up a proportional relationship between the actor figure and its immediate environment with confidence.

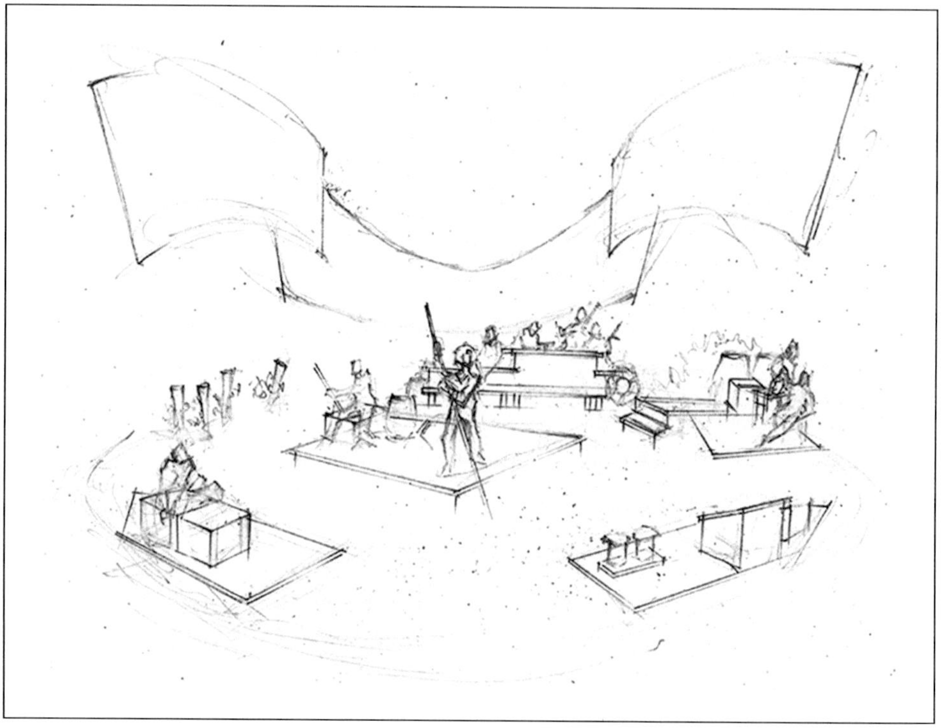

- Step 3:

  Draw more details to finalize your drawing. Make sure the added details not only complete the visual composition, but also work in line with perspective principles. Add shading and other drawing techniques to enhance the drawing.

Tip: Make a decision on where the key light comes from in your drawing and use all of the drawing techniques discussed in Chapter 6 to enhance it. In most cases, it will work better if you can work in "layers," which means establishing contrast among object groups at different position in depth.

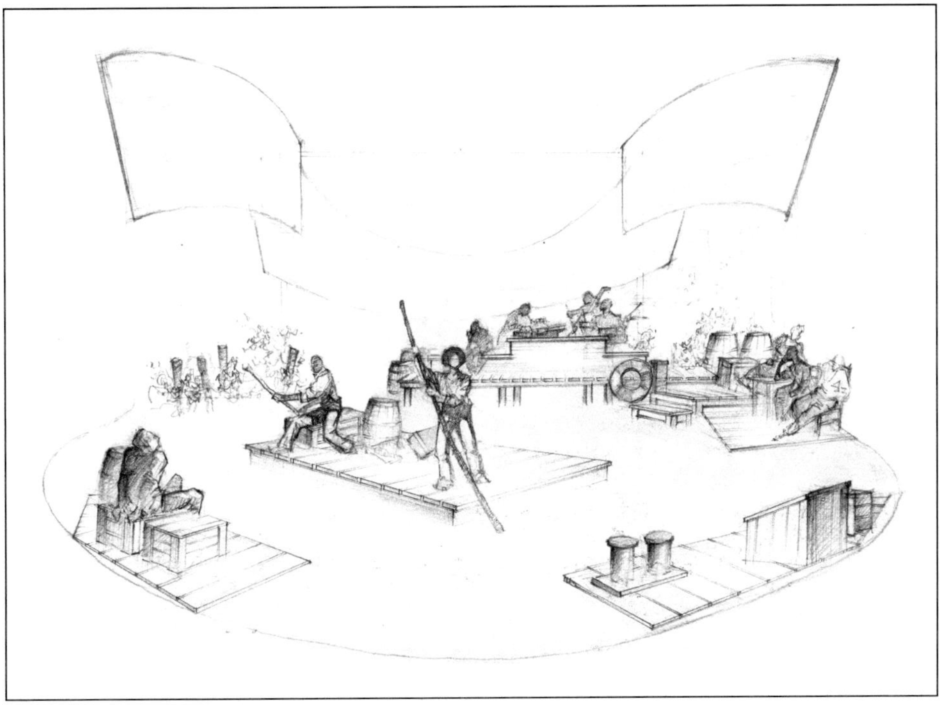

A DISCUSSION ON THUMBNAIL SKETCHES

Thumbnail sketches are rough quick sketches in small size. They allow a designer to explore various design compositions and style potentials without devoting too much time. By nature, they are sketches a designer draws for self-study. In most cases, they are not meant to be shared with others. So, they could be drawn really rough, without much consideration on presentational quality. The key is it still needs to be drawn with perspective in mind and to be kept in proportion. Drawing some thumbnail sketches to compare for compositional options is highly recommended before using any of the three perspective drawing methods discussed above in a real design process. I'm used to drawing my design thumbnail sketches in bound sketch books of 5" x 7" size. It helps to keep my design process record in hand, not to lose some valuable original ideas. Some design ideas which end up not working for one project might be good for another one later.

Below are examples of thumbnail sketches from my design files. A finished pencil sketch follows each thumbnail sketch to illustrate the relationship between the thumbnail sketch and the final design sketch.

BLUES TO AN ALABAMA SKY, True Color Theatre, Atlanta, 2009

Thumbnail Sketch:
Focus on space arrangement, basic shape and proportion. Some value contrast was added for clarification.

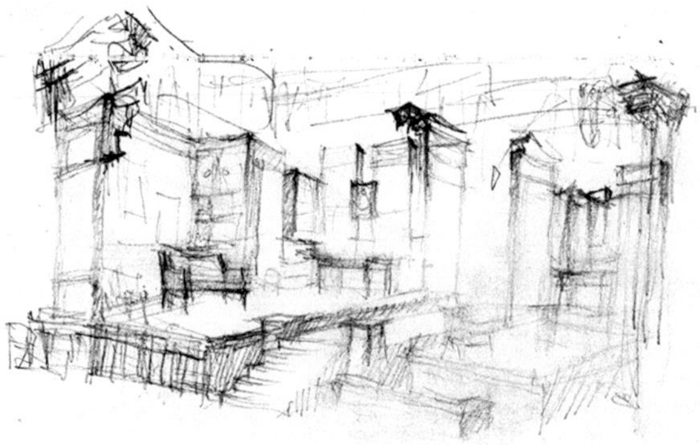

Finished Pencil Sketch:
Guided by a fully developed floor plan to work out the show's need of two apartments and part of the street, built up from the thumbnail sketch, clarify design details in consideration.

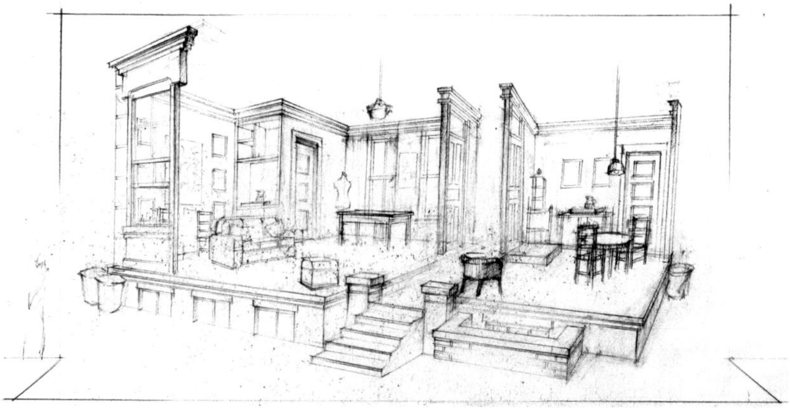

DIARY OF ANNE FRANK, Arrow Rock Lyceum Theatre, 2009

Thumbnail Sketch:

Work on space arrangement and shape composition.

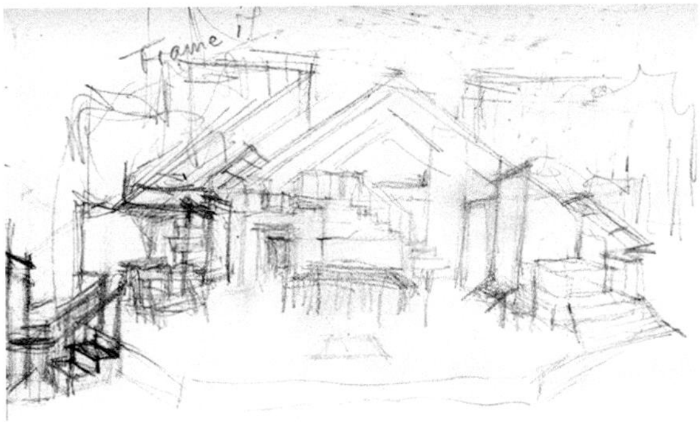

Finished Pencil Sketch:

Working from a fully developed floor plan to meet this show's complex needs in spacing arrangement, developed from the thumbnail sketch in basic composition to go with the overall situation set-up, add in more details to finish the set's look.

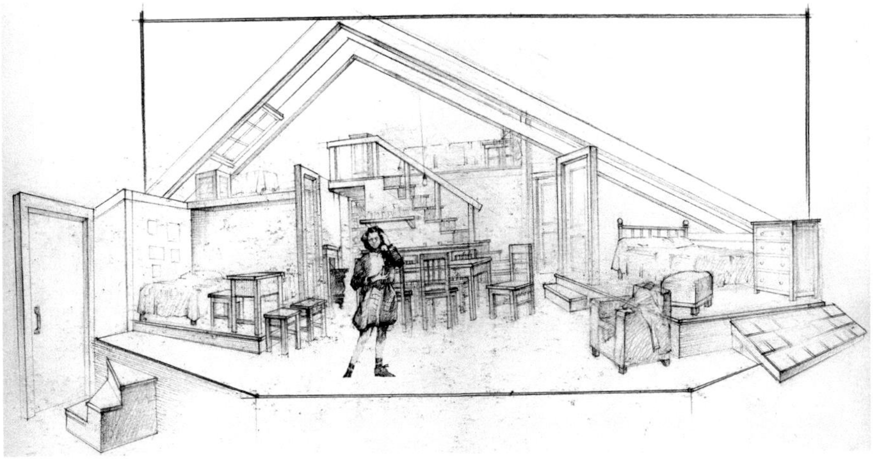

PETER PAN, Variety Theatre, 2013

Thumbnail Sketch:

Focus on composition and space arrangement to get some feel of a ship and satisfy the basic needs of the scene: levels, hidden place, big crowd movement.

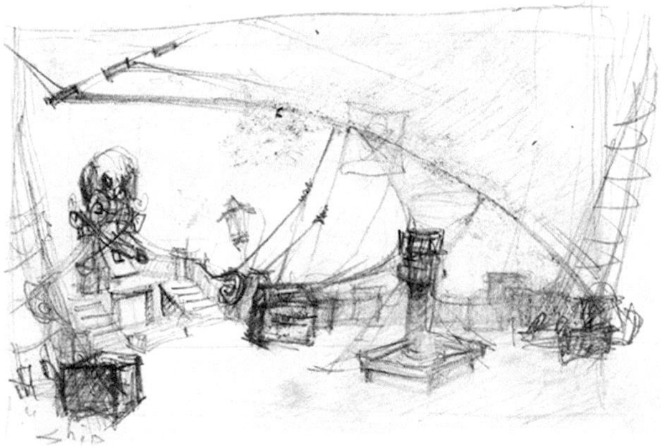

Finished Pencil Sketch:

Work from a fully developed floor plan, developed from the thumbnail sketch in basic space arrangement and composition to make sure all of the basic needs of this scene are met. Adjust proportion and add in more details to enhance the presentational quality.

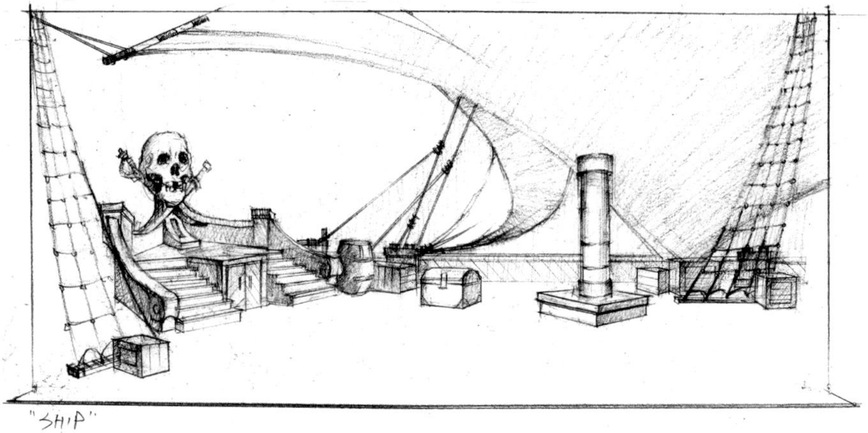

JANE EYRE, Mustard Seeds Theatre, 2013

Thumbnail Sketch:

Work on space arrangement and shape composition. Special attentions were paid to scene shifts from one location to another for this multi-location unit set.

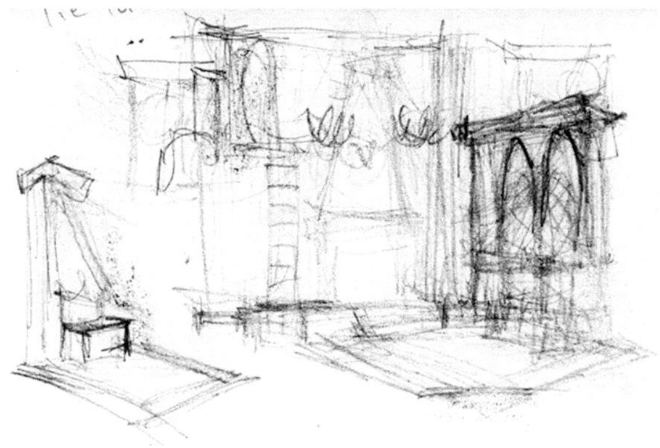

Finished Pencil Sketch:

Based on a fully developed floor plan which worked out all of the shifts between scenes. Referring to the compositions in the thumbnail sketch as visual guide lines, adjust and add in details to complete the design presentation.

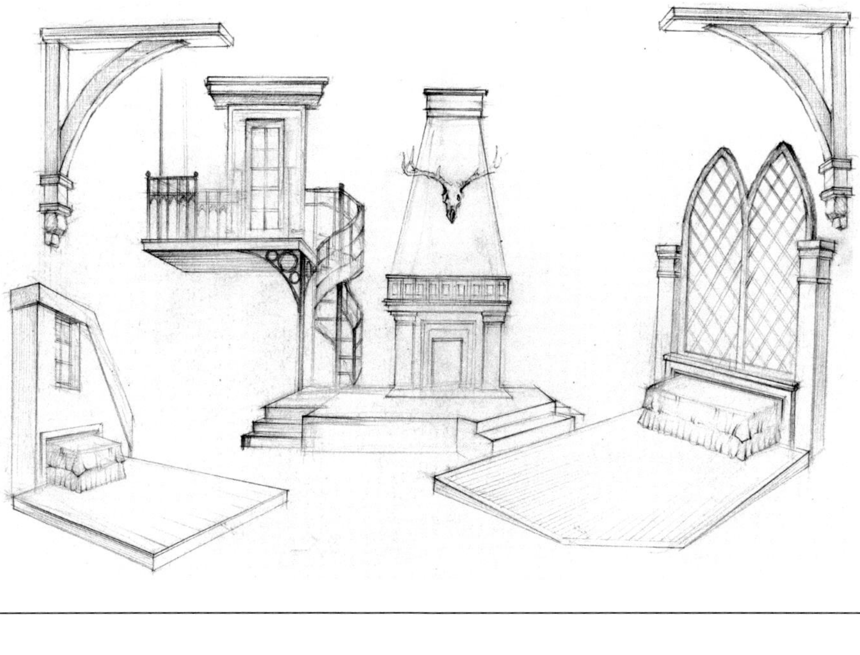

SPEED THE PLOW, New Jewish Theatre, 2012

Thumbnail Sketch:

Work on space arrangement and basic shape composition.

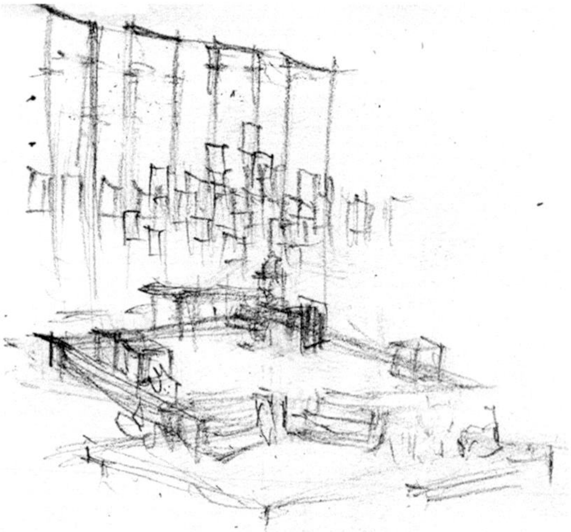

Finished Pencil Sketch:

Based on a fully developed floor plan with a space arrangement of two basic acting areas, referring to the thumbnail sketch in basic visual composition. Work in details to finish the design presentation.

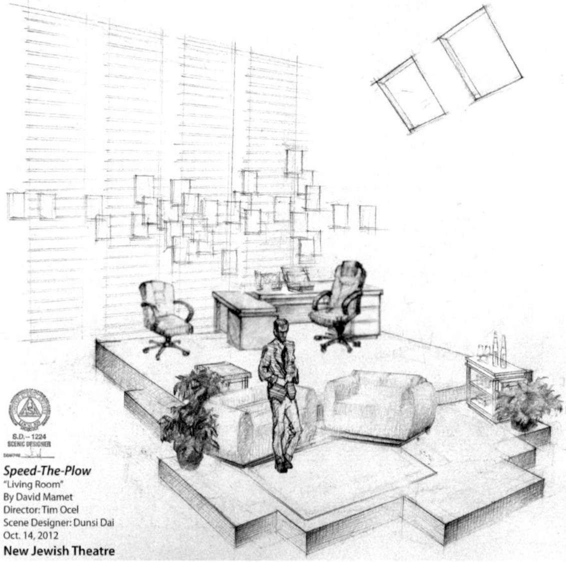

SIGHT UNSEEN, New Jewish Theatre, 2015

Thumbnail Sketch:

Work on a space arrangement and basic visual composition.

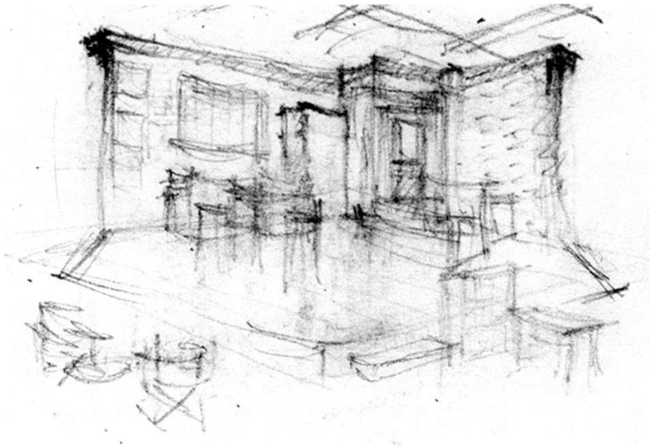

Finished Pencil Sketch:

Based on a fully developed floor plan. Developed from the thumbnail sketch in visual composition. Add in details to finish the set's general look with features.

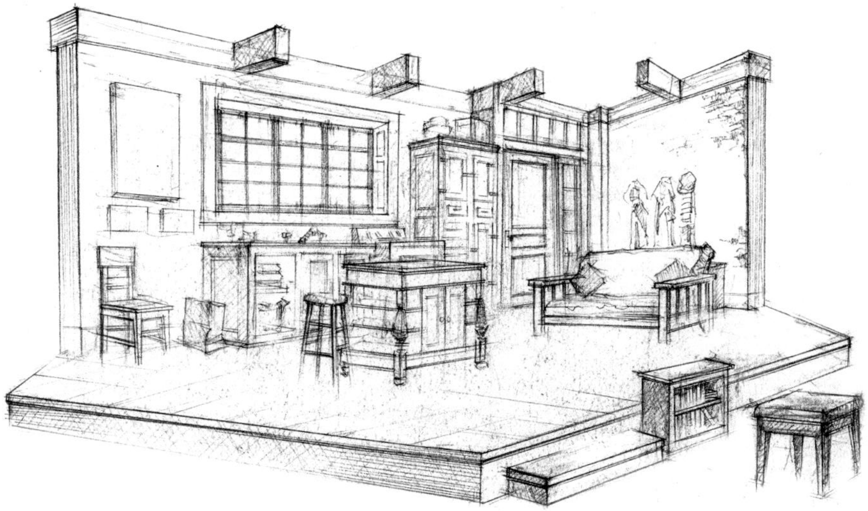

CHAPTER 9

DRAWING FIGURES IN PERSPECTIVE DRAWING

It is highly recommended to draw at least one actor figure in your perspective drawing. It helps to establish an important proportional reference as you move forward in the process. In most cases, designers tend to draw an actor figure with simple lines to save time. Sometimes, we draw more detailed actor figures to elevate the drawing's presentational quality.

HOW TO DRAW A FIGURE IN SIMPLE LINE

Since the drawing intends to be done fast, simple is better.

	• Step 1: Use your scale ruler to make a 6' high mark in the same scale used in your grid or frame.
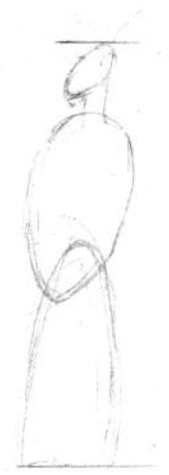	• Step 2: Rough in posture lines with the arm lines connected and the leg lines connected. This helps to control the gesture. Although the common head to body ratio is 1:7, you might want to make the ratio 1:7.5 to make the figure look more handsome.

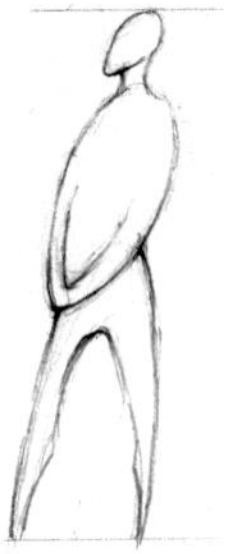	• Step 3: Adjust and clean up lines. Make some value variations with those lines to blow some "life" into this actor figure.

Tip: In most cases, you can use a line actor figure as your stock figure, and repeat it for all of the perspective drawings you are working on, since this figure only serves as a scaled reference. There's no need to create a new one for each drawing, unless you are looking for better presentation at the final stage of drawing.

HOW TO DRAW A FIGURE WITH MORE DETAILS

For a better presentational look, sometimes you may want to draw actors in your perspective drawing with more details.

	• Step 1: Use your scale ruler to make a 6' high mark in the same scale used as in your grid or frame.
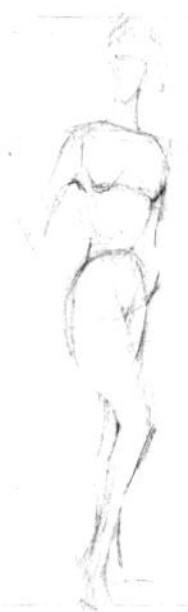	• Step 2: Rough in the basic posture, and keep the posture lines connected: left arm is connected with right arm through shoulder, the left leg is connected with the right leg at the hip, etc., so all of the major body parts are structured in a consistent gesture. While you are working on the posture, keep in mind that the head size to the total body height ratio is 1:7 (1:7.5 looks better).

	Also, keep in mind that clothes are just covers. The body under the clothes determines the basic look and posture. Thus, draw the body lines out first, adjust them to make them look right in proportion with the posture. There are three controlling elements that are deciding factors in composing a posture: head, shoulder, and hip. In most postures, these three major parts always tend to move slightly to the opposite direction compared with their neighbors in creating a feel of balance.
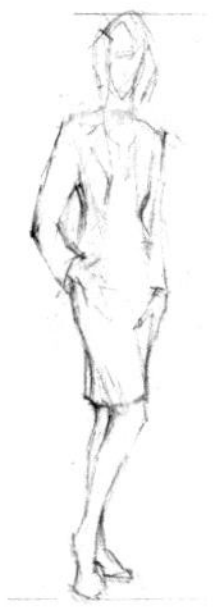	• Step 3: Cover the body with a costume. Pay special attention to those fabric folds at the joints. They will either enhance or spoil your drawing.
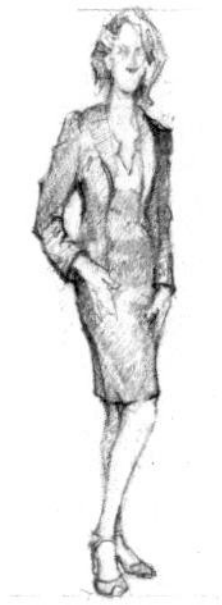	• Step 4: Clean up loose lines, put in selected details (don't overdo it). Decide key light direction and work out highlights and shadows.

Tip: The face is always eye-catching in a drawing. However, it is recommended that for your perspective drawing, you do not want to draw too many facial details for your reference figures. Just some hints of the eyes, maybe a little hint of the nose is enough. This practice not only speeds up your drawing process, but it can also make your drawing look more presentable and keep the focus on the set.

More drawing figure samples:
A MIDSUMMER NIGHT'S DREAM, St. Louis Black Rep, 2012

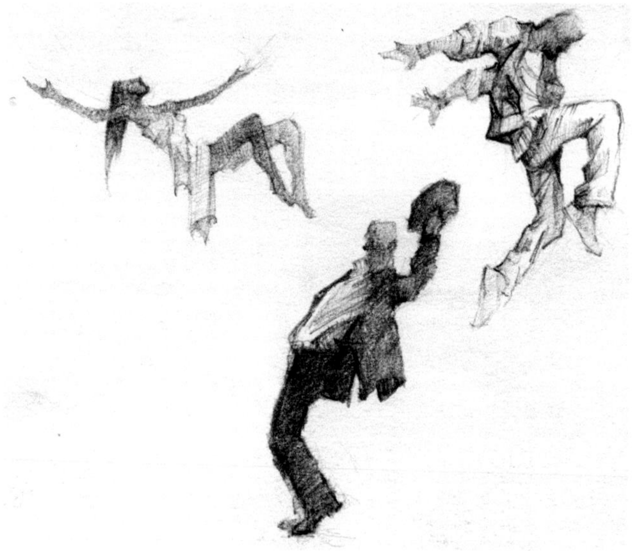

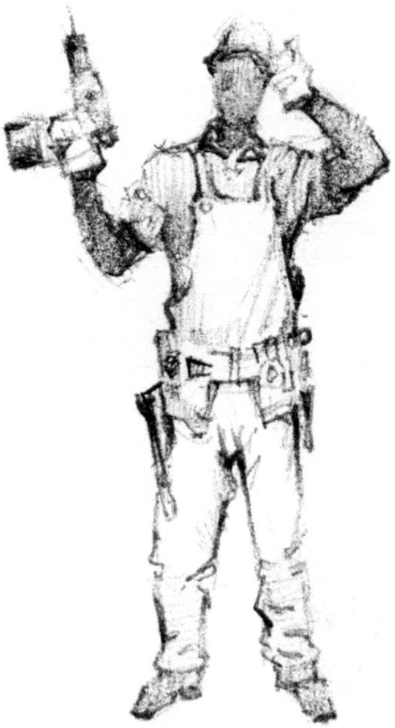

CHAPTER 10

PERSPECTIVE DRAWING PROJECTS

The following are three major projects used in my perspective drawing classes for years. They are class projects, designed to help students practice specific tasks in their learning process.

YOUR ROOM

This is a project aiming to practice perspective drawing with the Grid Method. "Your Room" means the room in which the student stays. In the case of college students, this is often the dormitory room or the apartment which they rent. This choice does not require much research, and all of the needed information (locations, measurements, details) is there with the student. They can get those quickly and easily when they need them, and concentrate on the drawing part of the project.

- Step 1:

  Use a scale ruler to draft a floor plan of the room in 1/2" scale. The floor plan needs to show the room layout and all of the major elements of the room in scale, including the size of the room, the locations of the window, the door, the closet, etc., as well as the locations of the major furniture pieces such as bed, desk, chair, etc. Grid the floor plan to match it with the grid size used in the perspective grid.
- Step 2:

  Use a straight ruler as a "cutter" to "cut" (cross) the floor plan to decide how to present this room (composition). While the student is required to do this project with the Grid Method, the student has options of doing this project either in one vanishing point perspective, or in two vanishing points perspective. The choice on how to "cut" the room will help to decide which perspective option ends up to be chosen.
- Step 3:

  Set up a perspective grid as discussed in Chapter 5. Pay attention to how to modify the grid to match the space's size and shape.

- Step 4:

  Rough the room into the perspective grid, based on the gridded floor plan and related visual researches (cell phone photos of the room work well). Match the wall/object's grid positions to their positions on the gridded floor plan. Put all furniture pieces in cube shapes to go along with the perspective grid in size and perspective angle.

- Step 5:

  Put in details. Add in set dressing (smaller objects which bring "life" and "character" into this space). Erase the perspective grid. Adjust and clean up the drawing to make it work better in proportion and perspective.

- Step 6:

  Establish a key light direction in the room and work on drawing techniques to further enhance the drawing. Keep reflective light in mind and avoid drawing solid black shadows. In most case, a hint of shadow at the corners and cut lines is enough to enhance the three-dimensional quality of the room and those objects in the room.

Tip: In order for this assignment to be more meaningful as a training process for beginning scene designers, a good Your Room project should not only show a handsome perspective drawing but should also show the character (the student) in this place. This does not require the students to draw themselves in the sketch. Instead, it asks to show the student's personal preferences, interests, hobbies, and lifestyle in the sketch to make this space stand out with "character": what does this room's owner like to do, who are his/her favorite movie/music stars, whether this is a tidy person or a messy one, etc. A successful project not only presents a handsome perspective drawing, but also gives enough clues to the viewers in answering questions of "Who are you?" "What kind of person lives here?"

VICTORIAN ROOM

This is a project used to practice the Frame Method. It could alternatively be done with the Grid Method, depending on the drawer's drawing skill level. This project emphasizes the process of drawing from serious research to complete a handsome perspective sketch. Every major piece in this project is required to have visual researches to back it up. This is a practice much closer to a real design situation that a scene designer faces every day.

Tip: Victorian is a period style with widely available research materials: in the library, on the internet, as well as in many old cities as represented by many historical buildings. Thus, the research process is less challenging to students (less time-consuming). The emphasis is on the process: drawing with serious period research.

A "Victorian Room" here really means an enclosed space in Victorian style, like a box set. Ideally, it could be the living room (drawing room, reception room), or the parlor. But it could also be done with any other room, such as the library room, dining room, kitchen, cellar, attic, etc. In one of my past classes, three students opted to draw a Victorian bathroom for this project. They came up with some great research and did very well on the project.

- Step 1:

  Research on Victorian style architecture, mostly interiors. Understand the features of Victorian style. Identify which type of room you would like to do for this project and collect related visual research.

- Step 2:

  Draw a rough floor plan of a Victorian house, including the room of choice. This will help the student to understand the logical position of the chosen room in the overall context of the house (life logic). It also helps to avoid pitfalls such as having windows set up on the "wrong side" of the room, etc.

- Step 3:

  Use a straight ruler to "cut" (cross) the chosen room on the floor plan to decide how to present it in a perspective drawing.

- Step 4:

  Draw some thumbnail sketches to work out a composition, based on the floor plan and the collected visual research. Modify the floor plan for better compositional options. Choose the one that works the best and use it as the visual composition guide to move forward.

- Step 5:

  Draw a scaled floor plan of the chosen room in 1/2" scale (or 1/4" scale). Draw only the area that you are going to do your perspective drawing. Use this floor plan as the basis to refer to your perspective drawing in proportional relationship.

- Step 6:

  Draw a reference frame with reference marks (based on the floor plan). Set your horizon line at 3' of the frame from the floor and draw a 6' tall actor figure in simple line right next to this reference frame.

- Step 7:

  Rough in the major parts of the room in basic shapes, guided by the chosen thumbnail sketch you created in Step 4. Use the reference frame and the reference actor figure to help to estimate the proportional relationships among the set pieces. Referring to the floor plan to further adjust the proportional relationship among the set pieces.

- Step 8:

  Adjust perspective angles and proportional relationship to make them "look right." Add details. When in question, apply the cube system. Keep checking with the reference frame marks and the reference actor figure for proportional reference. Remember to apply the perspective principles to the set pieces, depending on their positions on the floor plan (see Chapter 7 for details).

- Step 9:

  Establish a key light direction in the space. Apply shadow/highlight and other drawing techniques to finish this drawing.

A STREET CORNER

This is a project for practicing the Freehand with References Method. It could be done with the Frame Method as well, if the student chooses to do so.

> *Tip: Sketching an exterior perspective drawing could be challenging, compared with sketching an interior perspective drawing (a box set). Although all of the perspective elements and principles still apply, using multiple vanishing points is common in exterior perspective drawing. Because some buildings could be turned, the street might not have 90-degree turns, many buildings in larger sizes show numerous dimensional details. Generalizing selective details is called for and will help to make the drawing more workable.*

"A Street Corner" is another drawing from research project, which aims to enhance drawing abilities based on research from different resources. It is best to be done with Freehand with References Method.

- Step 1:

  Do visual research on a street corner you are interested in. Major elements that need to be considered are: its potential composition, the readable details, and the surface contrast in texture.

> *Tip: Drawing pencil sketches of the scene as part of the research process is encouraged because drawing from life helps the drawer to analyze, generalize, and understand the perspective relationship among the buildings and other objects involved in the scene. On the other hand, working from photographic research (taking pictures on the spot, scanning library books, researching photographs on the internet, etc.) works fine as well in most cases.*

- Step 2:

  Draw thumbnail sketches to work out some desired visual compositions, and choose the most satisfactory one as the compositional guide to develop further in next step.

- Step 3:

  Establish a horizon line position (the viewer's eye level). Rough in the street scene in basic shapes based on the chosen thumbnail sketch you created in Step 2, and adjust it guided by perspective principles.

- Step 4:

  Draw a reference actor next to a building with an easily comparable reference element (such as a door, a balcony with a handrail, a garden chair, etc.), and adjust the actor's size to make sure it is in proportion with the set elements next to him. For example, we know a regular door is with a 6'–8" high and 36" wide opening. Make your actor's size in proportion to this door accordingly.

- Step 5:

  Use this actor as the proportional reference point to further adjust the proportional relationship with other buildings to make them "look right" in proportion, and make sure all perspective principles are applied.

Tip: You will need to estimate a lot in this process. The keys to success are to trust your common sense with your trained experience in perspective drawing and always check back with the reference actor figure you established for proportional relationships.

- Step 6:

  Add details and make sure they work within the perspective relationship you have established and go along with perspective principles such as showing more details in the foreground and fading details for objects in the distance.

- Step 7:

  Establish a key light direction in your drawing. Add shading to work out highlight and shadow. Add visual texture to work out surface contrast.

A Street Scene Sketch Example:
A scene design sketch with a street scene: "Street", CINDERELLA, Houston Children Theatre Festival, 1994

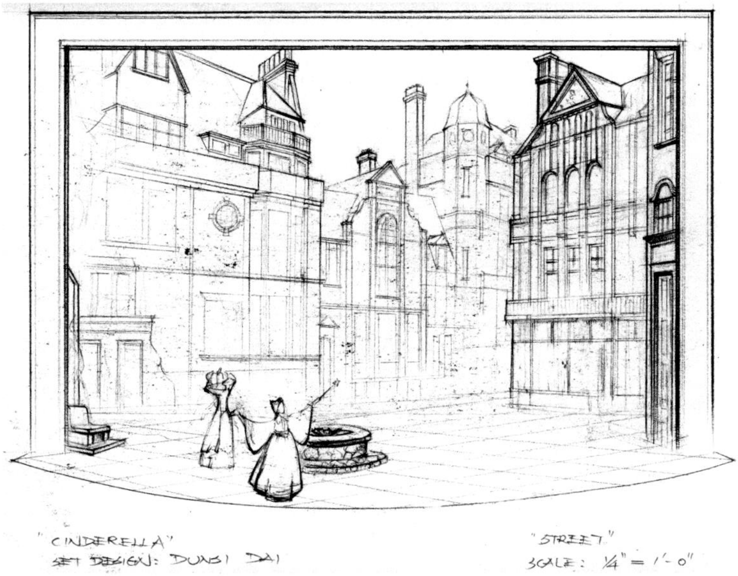

CHAPTER 11

THE NEXT STEP: EDIT AND DEVELOP PERSPECTIVE DRAWING IN PHOTOSHOP

Adobe Photoshop has become one of the most effective tools in the toolbox for today's designer. It also works very effectively in editing perspective drawings. I've been using Photoshop to edit my design sketches and renderings for years and have really enjoyed the convenience, flexibility, and the creative power that Photoshop has brought into my design studio. In my design practice, it helps me with speedy editing after working out hand-drawn perspective sketches, as well as to create editable set rendering in the next step.

The need to edit your perspective drawing happens every day in a scene design studio. It is expected. There are always new ideas, new suggestions, new feedbacks, and new tryouts popping up. Photoshop is the best tool for getting those done in a speedy way.

Photoshop gives a designer the freedom to:

- Draw only what is needed. Cut down those repetitive works on duplicating your drawing from one part to another. For example: For a symmetrical design, you could draw only half of the set; then, copy, flip what you drew, and put it in a mirror position within Photoshop to get a perfect matching symmetrical sketch done.

TARTUFFE, Mustard Seeds Theatre, 2010

The original pencil sketch:

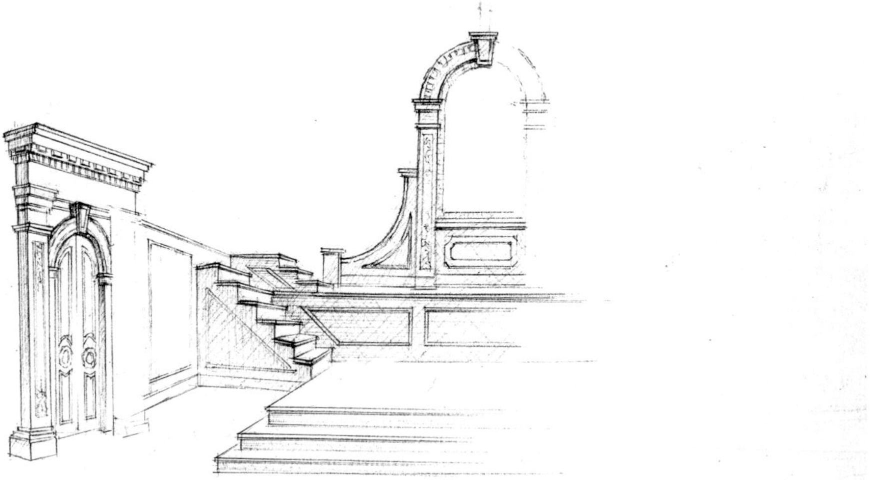

The finished sketch, after being worked in Photoshop:

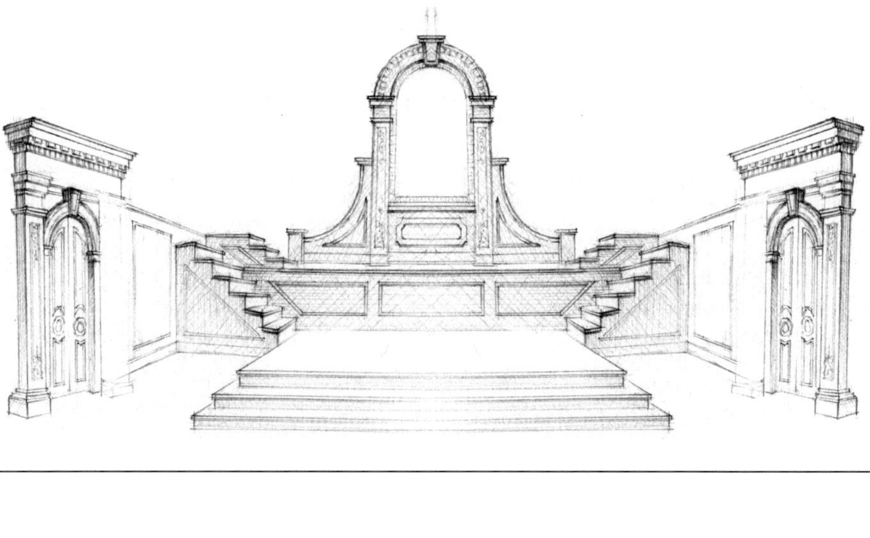

- When you are designing a show with multiple sets that have many shared elements in many scenes (like a unit set or a set with a false proscenium, and shared drops, or shared levels), instead of drawing a new sketch for every scene from scratch, you can draw a base set-up of your set with all of the stationary set pieces with pencil first, and scan your sketch into Photoshop. Then add/subtract shifted set pieces on different layers for each scene individually. After that, import those separated set pieces into the base drawing through turning on/off desired layers.

JANE EYRE, Mustard Seeds Theatre, 2013

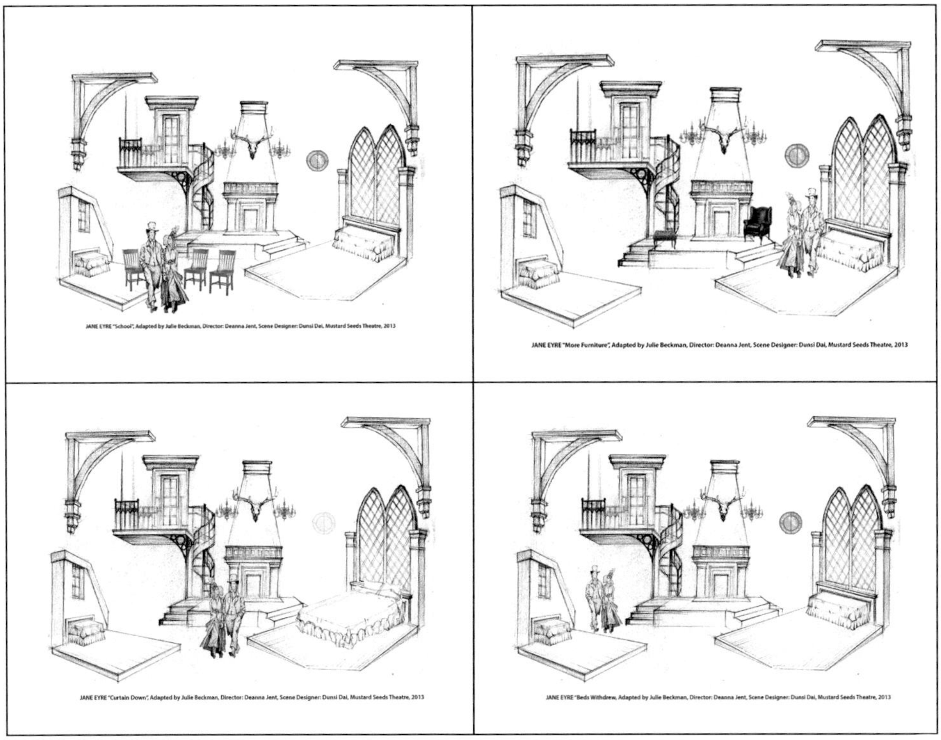

- Modify and enhance your perspective sketch with Photoshop's powerful features. Bring in your visual research into your set sketch directly.

OLD WICKED SONGS, New Jewish Theatre, 2016

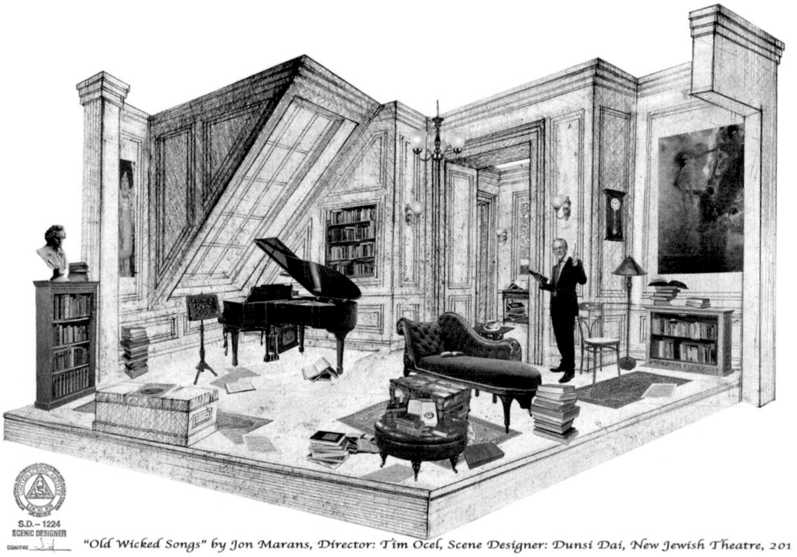

Then, render your perspective sketch with Photoshop to finish it as a set rendering.

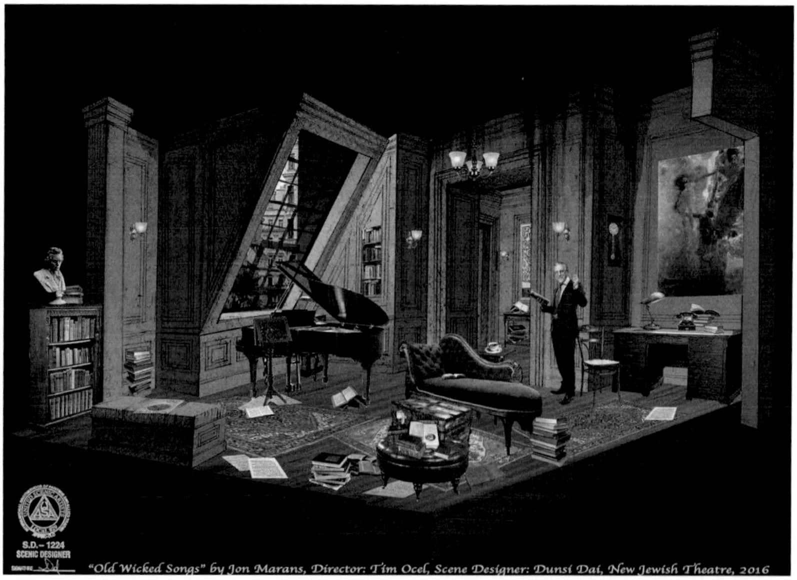

- Render a set from a perspective sketch to finish it as a colored set rendering with needed color and lighting information. Yes, Adobe Photoshop has developed into a fully powered digital rendering tool.

"Nursery," PETER PAN, Variety Theatre, 2013

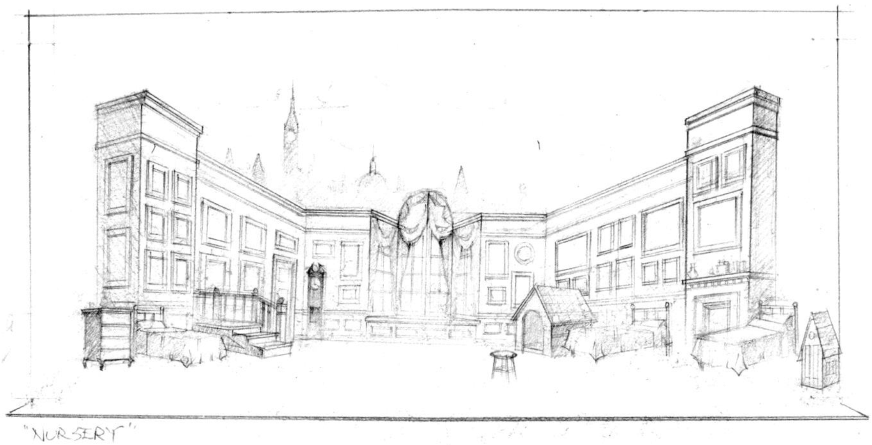

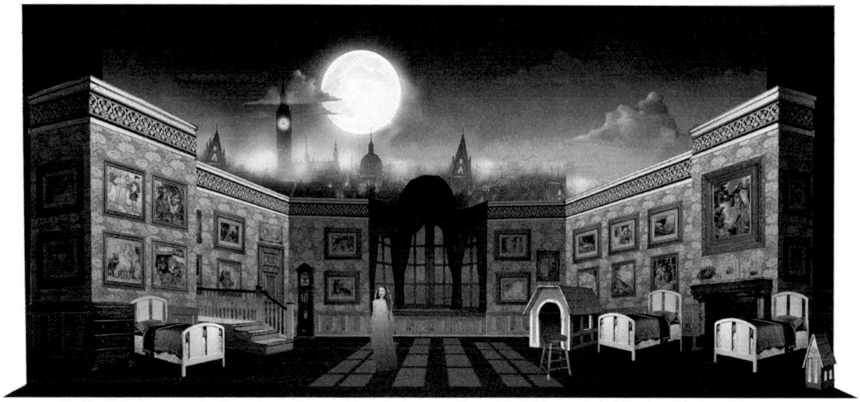

"Nursery", PETER PAN, By Carolyn Leigh, Director: Lara Teeter, Scene Designer: Dunsi Dai, Variety Theatre, 2013

To see this book's Photoshop set renderings in color, please log into the publisher's website at www.routledge.com/9780367860790.

This book focuses on perspective hand drawing only, because it has been written as a textbook for teaching perspective drawing to college students in a time frame of one semester. Thus, we will not discuss how to use Photoshop to edit perspective drawing and set rendering here.

On the other hand, after you master the perspective drawing methods discussed in this book, it is natural that you may want to move forward to take advantage of Photoshop's editing and rendering power to further enhance your ability to work with your perspective drawing and create a colored set rendering. Keep an eye out for my next book, *Practical Photoshop Guide for Theatrical Designers: Scene Design, Costume Design, Prop Design, Hair and Makeup Design.*

SUPPLEMENTARY MATERIAL

A SAMPLE CLASS SCHEDULE

(One semester: 16 weeks)

This sample class schedule is based on the class syllabus I have used at Webster University's Conservatory of Theatre Arts, with minor alternations.

Week 1: Introduction:

- Perspective Basic: Perspective Elements and Principles
- Material and Tools

Week 2: Cube System

- What is Cube System
- How Cube System Works
- Practice on "Drawing from Cube to Object"

Week 3: Grid Method I: One Vanishing Point Perspective

Project 1:"Draw Your Classroom with a One Vanishing Point Grid"

Project requirements:

Draw your classroom from research

Project steps:

- Research
- Floor plan
- Composition in thumbnail sketch
- Make a one vanishing point perspective grid
- Draw your classroom as a perspective sketch

Week 4: Grid Method II: Two Vanishing Points Perspective

Project 1 due

Project 2: "Your Room" Project

Project requirements:

- Research
- Floor plan
- Thumbnail sketches for composition

- Work out a two vanishing points perspective grid
- Draw perspective sketch with personal touch (depict a character in this room: personality, hobbies, what the character likes, etc.)

Week 5: Drawing Techniques: Value, Texture, Shading/Highlight, Use Eraser as Drawing Tool and Sketch Finishing

- Working in class on Project 2
- Project 2 is due at the end of the class

Week 6: Working with/Modifying Pre-made Grid

Project 3: Practice drawing from a pre-made grid

- Choose a student-designed show with floor plan and elevations as researched
- Use a pre-made grid to set up a perspective grid to work with. Adjust the grid as needed
- Use the floor plan and the perspective grid to lay the set in perspective
- Finish the sketch with pencil techniques enhancements

Week 7: Finish Project 3

- Working in class on Project 3
- Project 3 is due at the end of the class

Week 8: Frame Method

Project 4: "A Victorian Room"

Project requirements:

Draw a room in Victorian style from research

- Research
- Floor plan
- Thumbnail sketch composition
- Use the Frame Method to work out this perspective drawing (could be done with the Grid Method, if it is preferred)

Week 9: Break (Fall or Spring)

Week 10: Workshop I

Check on research, floor plan, work out a composition with thumbnail sketches

Week 11: Workshop II

Set up a Reference Frame. Rough in cubes. Drawing in progress.

Week 12: Workshop III

Continue working on Project 4: put in details and finishing touches

Project 4 is due at the end of the class

Week 13: "Freehand with References Method"

Project 5: "A Street Corner"

Draw a street corner from research

Project requirements:

Research

Thumbnail sketch for composition

Drawing with either Freehand with References Method, or Frame Method

Week 14: Workshop IV

Check on research and thumbnail sketch (for composition)

Rough in basic shapes, and establish references

Week 15: Workshop V

Continue working on Project 5: put in details and finishing touches

Project 5 is due at the end of the class

Week 16: Projects Review

Downloadable PDF Pre-made Grid Files from the Publisher's Website:

(www.routledge.com/9780367860790)

Number	File Name	Paper Size	Note
1	Figure W.1	11" x 17"	One Vanishing Point Grid in PDF
2	Figure W.2	8.5" x 14"	One Vanishing Point Grid in PDF
3	Figure W.3	8.5" x 11"	One Vanishing Point Grid in PDF
4	Figure W.4	11" x 17"	Two Vanishing Points Grid in PDF
5	Figure W.5	8.5" x 14"	Two Vanishing Points Grid in PDF
6	Figure W.6	8.5" x 11"	Two Vanishing Points Grid in PDF

INDEX